The Burden of Prophecy

THE BURDEN OF PROPHECY

Poetic Utterance in the Prophets

of the Old Testament

Albert Cook

Southern Illinois University Press

Carbondale and Edwardsville

Library of Congress Cataloging-in-Publication Data

Cook, Albert Spaulding.
The burden of prophecy : poetic utterance in the prophets of the
Old Testament / Albert Cook.
p. cm.
Includes bibliographical references and index.
1. Bible. O.T. Prophets—Criticism, interpretation, etc.
2. Bible. O.T. Prophets—Language, style. 3. Bible. O.T.
Psalms—Criticism, interpretation, etc. 4. Bible. O.T. Psalms—
Language, style. 5. Bible. O.T. Ecclesiastes—Criticism,
interpretation, etc. 6. Bible. O.T. Ecclesiastes—Language,
style. I. Title.
BS1505.2.C65 1996
224'.06—dc20   96-17804
ISBN 0-8093-2083-5 (alk. paper)   CIP

The paper used in this publication meets the minimum requirements of
American National Standard for Information Sciences—Permanence of Paper
for Printed Library Materials, ANSI Z39.48-1984. ∞

To Don and Bev Coleman

Ointment and perfume rejoice the heart:
So *doth* the sweetness of a man's friend by hearty counsel.

Proverbs 27.9

Contents

Acknowledgments

I SHOULD LIKE to thank those persons who commented on the manuscript of this book, Kenneth Dauber, Michael Wade, Susan Slyomovics, and Irving Massey; and members of the audience at SUNY Buffalo, where I gave an early version of the Isaiah chapter as a lecture. I am also grateful to Brown University for steady logistical and intellectual support during the process of writing and especially to my ever-resourceful research assistant, Blossom S. Kirschenbaum. I should also like to thank John Wilson at SIU Press for skillful and attentive editing. My wife, Carol, as always, provided the deeply grounded support of reassurance and wisdom.

The Burden of Prophecy

1

Introduction

ALONG TIME ago, I projected a book on biblical poetry that found its
expression in *The Root of the Thing: A Study of Job and the Song of
Songs*. Intermittently, I wrote about other parts of the Bible: about Pen-
tateuchal narrative, briefly, in *The Meaning of Fiction* and about historiographic assumptions underlying biblical practice in *History/Writing*.
Further, in "Prophecy and the Preconditions of Poetry" (in *Soundings*),
I set the biblical practice of poetry into a larger context of comparable
poetry with some religious orientation, while attempting some charac-
terizations and drawing some distinctions. Here I turn, finally, to the
tonic range of biblical prophecy and to its "burden," a word that has
been adapted into English to mean the kind of message that the biblical
prophet conceived himself to be uttering.

The biblical sense of "burden" is listed separately in the Oxford English Dictionary, but it is difficult for an English speaker to dissociate
the word from most of the other senses: a load, a duty, a crop, a musical
accompaniment, a refrain, a chief theme or idea, that which is borne in
the womb, and even (the burden of) a proof. There are elements, situational and metaphorical, in prophetic utterance that would validate
such extensions of the word. The Hebrew *maśśā* is used to mean the
burden of an ass or a camel, though when it is derived from *naśāh*, "lift,"
it more strongly suggests a raising motion than does the English word
"burden," which is derived from "bear." Gesenius, indeed, lists *maśśā*
in the prophetic sense as a separate word, indicating that its main use
is "utterance" or "oracle," an emphasis that the Septuagint translation
reinforces by rendering it with the Greek words for "speech" and "oracle," *rhēma* and *orama*.[1] It also renders the word, however, as "something received or taken up," *lēmma*. This lends support to the "burden"
side of the Hebrew word and allows both senses—that of a load and
that of a raised voice—to blend somewhat as they do in the English

1

word and, for that matter, in the situation of the Hebrew prophet, whose voice is raised and whose freight of duty is indeed hard to carry.

In looking at the fusion of poetic with scriptural thinking in the prophets and wisdom writers, I focus here on the details, on the quick of the thinking, on their thematic concentrations, and on the posture they assume to orient them in their utterance. I take the view that a deep associability of theme and prophetic posture justifies lumping together under the name Isaiah the three prophets whom modern commentators have long ascertained were active over a span of two centuries or so. Even traditional ascriptions that have far less historical justification—like ascribing Ecclesiastes and Proverbs to a Solomon who lived nearly a millennium before they were composed or calling David the author of the Psalms—still have some thematic relevance. When we are dealing with cases like Jeremiah and Ezekiel, whose prophecies might reasonably have been uttered within the lifetime of a single prophet, the question is moot whether or not the person of that name wrote every line in the book so ascribed. Even the ascription of Lamentations to Jeremiah, which goes back to the Septuagint—at least as far back as the second century B.C.E.—while not usually accepted as fact, does have the justification of strong thematic and historical congruence. I look, therefore, only incidentally at the layerings of literary form and rhetorical purpose that modern commentators have discerned in each of the poetic books of the Old Testament that I discuss.

Homer, Confucius, the poets of the Confucian anthology, and the authors of the Zend Avesta and the Rig Veda are variously endowed with an authority empowered by the instituted religious thinking of their times, and all rest stably in the reassurances provided by their particular contexts. The Hebrew prophets, however, come forward and present themselves as open to the momentary utterances of God.[2] This God is not primarily an image or a symbol; the Hebrew Yahweh is a force manifesting himself in developing history.[3] In that dangerous situation, the prophet remains open directly to God and gets a continually renewed verbal authority and power from that flow. Since the prophet is commenting on the constantly changing flow between God and people, every utterance, while formed in reference to the basic values of righteousness and the law and in measured analogy to such defining tribal experiences as the Exodus, takes on the nature of a progress report rather than a finally poised formulation. In radical distinction to other religious poetry, Hebrew prophecy rises from and refers to a complex and specific occasion. The prophet is always testing the status of the covenantal relationship between the Hebrew kingdom and God that serves as the fundamental integrating force and definition of the prophet's society. According to George E. Mendenhall, "The messages of the prophets are essentially indictments of Israel for breach of covenant." Mendenhall specifies the complexity of this relationship:

> The covenant at Sinai was the formal means by which the semi-nomadic clans, recently emerged from state slavery in Egypt, were bound together in a religious and political community. The text of that covenant is the Decalogue. Since a covenant is essentially a promissory oath, it is only in this way that a social group could be made responsible to new obligations. Furthermore, it is only in this way (excluding overwhelming coercive force) that a legal or political community could and did expand, to include other already existing social units. . . . The covenant relationship itself may very well be regarded as a guarantee of freedom from every other political suzerainty.[4]

This covenantal society in its tensile progressions called for a figure like the prophet to express its deepest aspirations and urge it to be faithful to its religious orientation. This function is at once delicate and powerful, given the nature of the society, as Mendenhall explains: "The lateness of kingship in Israel is not due to the primitive nature of Israelite culture, but the opposite—it had succeeded well enough during those years to make any alternative seem foolish. . . . The related prophetic condemnation of the king is not then simply a foolhardy venture of a malcontent, but rather the verdict of a Supreme Court (or rather of his representative) for violation of the constitution."[5] Elsewhere, Mendenhall analyzes the nature of the covenant from a somewhat different angle:

> The subjection of individuals and groups to a non-human Overlord by covenant, and the solidarity of the newly formed community meant that they could and did reject the religious, economic, and political obligations to the existing network of political organizations. By this process they became "Hebrews." The religious

community of early Israel created a contrast between the religious and the political aspects of human culture which had been inseparable in the idea of the "divine state" or the "divine kingship," because a complete identification of religious with political authority and obedience, so characteristic of ancient and modern paganism, became impossible. The early community created a concept of obedience to norms which took precedence over the demands of any monopoly of force, and which was regarded as binding upon the state when it was finally established with Saul and David.[6]

The prophets extend, stretch, and simultaneously subvert and uphold this "new order." At the same time, they may be seen as deeply conservative supporters of the "law," the *torah* that is prevailingly religious rather than judicial in origin. For the past century and a half, commentators have occasionally interpreted the prophets as exhibiting currents of ideas that would have developed earlier than those in the Pentateuch.[7] However, the prophet's relation to the society is complex enough to include both "charismatic" and "institutional" elements, to use the terminology of Max Weber. The role of the prophet comprises aspects of both marginality and centrality, and it at least partially echoes the "cult" channeling of shamanistic and ecstatic functions exercised by the oracle-givers of neighboring societies in Mesopotamia, Canaan, and elsewhere.[8] Yet, in Israel the role of the prophet is an idealized and central one; as the statement attributed to Moses at an earlier time declares, "Would God that all the Lord's people were prophets" (Num. 11.29).[9]

The defining posture out of which the prophetic utterances arose is in place by the time of the earliest literary prophets, Amos and Hosea. Their role is threatened by the split of the kingdoms. It is threatened still more for their successors when the Southern Kingdom goes under. But this catastrophe also deepens and reasserts the possibility of national fulfillment across the generations of increasing stress, exile, and return.

We cannot approach the imaginative and cognitive reach of the biblical prophets if we do not take account of how their utterances reverberate through this particular complex context of communication. Much recent discussion of biblical prophecy has been aimed at demonstrating the literary coherence and subtlety of its poetic practices or else at deducing its particular situational locus, its *Sitz im Leben*, within its society. This is all to the good, though there are other questions to be asked about its communicative dimensions. What is this poetry about, and how does it work? Or, to adopt the term that Kenneth Dauber has applied to the Bible, what are the reference points of its relationality?[10] This term, like Martin Heidegger's *Bezug*, emphasizes the dynamic connection built into the utterance through the speaker's awareness of what the audience expects the speaker to assume. And at the same time, another sense of relation touches on the notion of a dimension of narrativity (many prophets do intermittently tell their own stories) implied in the historical rootedness of the utterance. Certainly, the prophet is not framing private responses to intimate events, nor inditing a resonant legend, nor working out a cosmology that involves a restructuring of the past. These are occupations of poets in our tradition but not in that of biblical prophecy.

The prophet, the people, and God are caught up in the prophetic pouring forth and in the dynamic interdependence of urgent revelation. If we think of a triangle with the prophet, the people, and their God standing at the three corners, it is a triangle of forces under constant motion and constant pressure. The words of the prophet, to continue this triangle metaphor, enunciate what is happening along the vectors that connect one point to another. Most discussion tends to freeze one of the corners of this triangle: to ask who this God is and so write about the theology of the prophet; or to ask what specific, or more general, situation the people finds itself in and so delineate historical circumstances; or to broach anthropological definitions by asking what the role of the prophet is.[11] All of these activities are not only unavoidable; they are crucially contributory to an understanding of the text, just as is conventional literary description of its coherences. But all these activities are also preliminary to addressing the burden of prophetic utterance.

Typically, the prophet, carrying reports about God, directly addresses the people; but sometimes, in Ezekiel and elsewhere, he reports "the word of God" directly. In Micah 6–7, the prophet voices a dialogue between God and the people. "O my people, what have I done unto thee," God complains (6.3). "Wherewith shall I come before the Lord?"

the people answer with their own question (6.6). And the prophet replies, "He hath showed thee, O man, what *is* good" (6.8). This three-way alternation is the first of the cumulative alternations lasting to the end of the book.

The transfers from God to prophet to people are transfers of power. The performative dimension of language, elaborately sketched by J. L. Austin, may be extended to the power relations underlying language and triggered by it.[12] As Pierre Bourdieu has delineated them, these power relations are constantly present, through many dimensions, in any act of utterance. As Bourdieu says about the social siting and power dynamics of all speech, "through the medium of the structure of the linguistic field, conceived as a system of specifically linguistic relations to power based on the unequal distribution of linguistic capital (or, to put it another way, of the chances of assimilating the objectified linguistic resources), the structure of the space of expressive styles reproduces in its own terms the structure of the differences which objectively separate conditions of existence."[13] These "linguistic relations to power" are necessarily quite complex in the modern societies to which Bourdieu mainly directs his attention. But the starker and simpler conditions of the biblical prophet, if measured by such a sociolinguistic calculus, reveal these relations not as "unequal" but as performing a dialectical turn upon the question of equality. The prophet is unequal to the king as his subject, but the prophet's access to God also makes the king unequal to the prophet. God, as always in this context, is the deciding term of the equation.[14]

The constant danger faced by the prophet and his resourceful adaptiveness are well characterized by Bourdieu's further formulation: "The legitimate language no more contains within itself the power to ensure its own perpetuation in time than it has the power to define its extensions in space. Only the process of continuous creation which occurs through the unceasing struggles between the different authorities who compete within the field of specialized production for the monopolistic power to impose the legitimate mode of expression can ensure the permanence of the legitimate language and of its value, that is, of the recognition accorded to it." In his "unceasing" struggles, the prophet must draw power from the people, itself derived through a power from God: "Relations of communication are always, inseparably, power relations which, in form and content, depend on material or symbolic power accumulated by the agents (or institutions) involved in these relations and which, like the gift or the potlatch, can enable symbolic power to be accumulated."[15]

Under these pressures, the prophet's utterance carries out, in J. L. Austin's terms, a performative act. Christening a ship—Austin's example—only happens performatively if the designated person breaks the champagne on the hull and says, "I christen you the *Columbia*." The vast fabric of social power relations is thereby touched upon, because the empowered person is empowered by someone; typically, she is a representative of a subsociety of ship launchers, naval or marine personnel, and the like, and the person or persons who choose her are themselves put forward and empowered to do so by those relations. As is true, though far more complexly, in prophetic utterance, many strands of social *habitus* here converge.[16] These include the gender expectations that dictate that the christener be a woman and the acculturative conventions of prestige dictating that champagne, a celebratory alcoholic beverage originally of foreign origin, be employed along with the appropriate words. Grape juice will not do nor will soda pop. Even the name of the ship is subject to conventions, and it will be dictated by a sense of appropriateness connected to the celebration of power. Names like *Stinky*, *Davy Jones' Locker*, and the like will not do—as they might do for a pleasure boat advertising the privacy of its owner's vacation from power structures. And the appropriateness of the ship's name can, on occasion, be challenged in the political arena; such was the case when the proposal to christen an atomic submarine *Corpus Christi* was protested by concerted groups who rejected the idea that doing so would honor the Texas city of that name, because the name derives from a central figure and event in Christian ritual, and they felt that the association of that holy name with an engine of destruction was blasphemous.

In such initially simple cases, and in those of high complexity, the whole social fabric as it carries along its activities through utterances is a tapestry of empowering designations about who may speak and under what circumstances. Age, preparation, ethnic identity, gender, assigned role, personal capacity, reputation, and other factors permute to situate and authorize the power relations of language. Yet it should not be forgotten that the constative dimension of any meaningful utterance cannot disappear. In Frege's terms, the sense of a statement—and much of its reference too—accompanies the fact of its assertion.

There also obtain what Austin calls "felicity conditions." So if I, a man, were to slip into the shipyard and break a bottle of champagne on a hull, uttering the words "I christen you the *Columbia*," the performative act will not have taken place. Its felicity conditions will have misfired. But the constative sense of the utterance remains what it is, and that constative sense would include a reference to the (unfulfilled) conditions of the social context of ship christening.

The Hebrew prophet of the times before and after the fall of Jerusalem delivers utterances that have a performative or perlocutionary, and also illocutionary, intention: uttered by someone empowered by stressful and constantly tested conditions, they are aimed at getting the Israelites to change heart and change their ways. The prophet urges this by spelling out in compelling fashion particular dynamisms along the vectors of the interactive triangle prophet-God-people. Comparing this action to the christening of a ship throws into relief the thrust, and also the uncertainty, of the situation. We know at once whether the ship was christened or not, whereas only the future will tell, one way or the other, whether the felicity conditions were present to effectuate what the prophet's words are performing. One could know whether the convergence of requisite features had taken place only after the fact and then not definitively, even though the hope of effectuating a turn of events is built into the verse as its enabling condition. Otherwise, why speak? Threat and appeal and vision, as conditions of utterance, all come into play; but how they will play out—the crucial question—is what is radically deferred.

The heavy bearing of a set of historical circumstances upon the prophets plays a special role in their work. The prophets constantly and directly refer to historical circumstances. Their successors, classed under the different rubric of wisdom writers, may be said to modulate their way beyond such direct references to the more normal literary posture of situational echo and yet still to depend on a prophetic template for urgency and focus. That is my justification for including Psalms and Ecclesiastes in this book. The kings are real and contemporary in Amos, First Isaiah, and Jeremiah, but they are metaphoric in Ecclesiastes and the Song of Songs, while the writer of the Book of Job schematizes a situation set in the past of a millennium beforehand. Dynasties are lined up in the Book of Daniel for a retrospective, somewhat fictionalized history.

After the time of such preliterary prophets as Nathan and Elijah, prophetic utterance comes through five large periods, each determined by a special set of circumstances. In the first period—that of First Isaiah, Amos, Hosea, Micah, and Habakkuk—the Northern Kingdom, progressively threatened for centuries by larger neighbors, reaches its dissolution in 721 B.C.E. at the hands of Sargon of Assyria. An overwhelming preoccupation with the phases of this threat engages these prophets. In the second period—that of Jeremiah, but also later, by a crucial decade or so, of Ezekiel—the Southern Kingdom, where Jerusalem is located, caught between Egypt and the still more powerful Babylon, is attacked by Nebuchadnezzar and finally undergoes destruction in 596. By the time of the literary prophets, the contemporary Egypt had become only one among many geopolitical factors, and it will not resume an important role till the time of the Seleucids (312–129).

With the Babylonian conquest, the whole of an autonomous Israel disappears. The complications leading up to that catastrophe and its immediate aftermath call upon these prophets for stressful assimilation, and the surviving Israelites are exiled progressively to various locations in the Babylonian Empire. In the third period, that of the exile—into which Ezekiel overlaps—the circumstances are simple but dire: now the prophet focuses on a hope of ultimate political restoration, a restoration that can only happen if it accords with a moral justification, or at least pardon, through Yahweh. This is the time of Second Isaiah.

The fourth period, after the Persian supremacy begins in 538, is the time of Zechariah, Haggai, and Malachi, as well as Third Isaiah. Israel is restored but in the condition of existing under the Persian yoke as a province of the Persian empire. The prophets are caught up in the dialectic of that dependent existence. This empire in its administration exhibits an ambivalent mixture of cruelty and benevolence, as we learn from the range of actions and policies recounted by Herodotus. A strong picture of vacillating benevolence comes through as well in the historical account provided by Ezra and Nehemiah, beginning with Cyrus's encouragement for the rebuilding of the Temple (Ezra 1–3). At the same time, a sense of cruelly arbitrary overlordship—the Persian not qualitatively different from the Babylonian—presides over the centuries-later retrospective conception of the books of Esther and Daniel. In the fifth period, the domination by distant powers has further settled into a fact of some centuries' duration. The wisdom writers and even the psalmists all largely precede the Maccabees, whose revolt against Antiochus Epiphanes, beginning about 166, overshadows the Book of Daniel. That book presents the picture of a desperate struggle against overwhelming dominance, although from a "future" perspective on the figure Daniel in the Babylonian and Persian Empires portrayed in that book written four centuries later.

The pressure of the historical circumstances in the first four periods is such that the prophet feels endangered and exposed in the here and now. This sense appears throughout the writings of the prophets and, notably, in the self-reference of the prophets themselves, beginning with Amos's complex depiction of his own circumstances and Hosea's allegorization of his marital life. The self-reference continues and expands in the protracted accounts by Isaiah and later by Jeremiah of their own particular circumstances. Such autobiographical writings are extraordinary in the biblical context and beyond it. They constitute perhaps the earliest autobiographical writings in human utterance.[17]

Israel, from the beginning, was dwarfed by the giant kingdoms that surrounded her at some distance, threatening her and invading her over the whole period of the literary prophets. But at the same time, her God, a figure of constantly unfolding development and intimate moral force, stood in overmastering contradistinction to the gods in the elaborate pantheons of these powerful neighbors. The narrative thread of Genesis involves the progressive distinction of the core of the chosen people from other peoples; and in the Exodus, the political nation of Israel undertakes gradual self-definition by separating itself from its vassalage to the powerful New Kingdom of Egypt, a long-term act or phase that is retained as legendized history for constant reference in the literary prophets. Political struggles here remain religious ones, and from Samson to Jezebel the Israelites undergo military threats that function also as threats to religious autonomy. The foreign gods in the prophets correlate with the foreign incursions—except that Israel's wars against such neighbors as the Philistines do not have the apocalyptic force of her unequal struggles against the Akkadians, Syrians, Assyrians, Babylonians, and Persians.

These prophecies, written prevailingly in verse, cast themselves in accordance with a prosody that takes as its main feature a parallelism of members, in which everything in some way gets said twice; it is as though the constant repetition provides a reassurance for the prophet who stands forth to speak under this future-oriented uncertainty, under constant personal and public danger. In this form, the second half of a verse (B) must in some way repeat what was said in the first half (A). The repetition-in-variation gathers the power of the utterance and constantly underscores it.

This simple doubling form permits a range of poetic identities and contrasts, especially in the dynamic forward thrust with which it is typically handled. Though the parallelism must carry in some form from one half of the verse to the other, the fact that it often carries further and that its modes of repetition vary makes its boundary uncertain. To continue a parallel element, then, stands as an omnipresent possibility at every point in a stretch of Hebrew verse.

Even in an early prophet like Micah, the form can get expansive within the compass of a single verse (5.4):[18]

>   a   b   c   d
> (A1) And he shall stand and feed in the strength of the Lord
> *ve ʿāmad ve rāʿāh beōz Adonai*
>
>   a   b   c   d
> (A2) In the majesty of the name of the Lord his God,
> *bi geʾôn šēm Adonai ʾElōhāv*
>
>   a
> (B1) And they shall abide:
> *ve yašāvû*
>
>   a   b   c   d
> (B2) For now shall he be great unto the ends of the earth.
> *kī ʿatah yigdal ʿadʾāphse āreṣ*

It should be noted that, omitting the particle-like prepositions and conjunctions, there is just one Hebrew word for each of the thirteen elements in this pair of bipartite lines, a single verse. The verse expands on the formal base of matching parallelism in which statements are repeated. "He shall stand" is repeated in "they shall abide"; "the strength of the Lord" is picked up by "the majesty of the name of the Lord his God." The whole statement A1–A2 is roughly equivalent to the whole statement of B1–B2, the first half of the verse to the second half. Details of the statement tend to follow along the lines of the obligatory matchings. "Stand" entails and is equivalent to "feed," an action (feeding the flocks) derived from and guaranteed by a "strength" that is necessarily that of the Lord. The Lord is "his God" because of such actions, which his "name" implies. In God's very name is a "majesty" that is equivalent to, and an aspect of, "strength." "Stand" also equals "abide," the beginning of the first pair of hemistichs matching the beginning of the second. All this amounts to "be great," an expression that matches the people, seen in the collective singular ("he," A1) or the plural ("they," B1), the singular and the plural thereby matched. And "be great" correlates with "strength" and "majesty," the people thereby coordinated with God.

The individual terms are condensed, each packed with a range of senses, as is indicated by an alternate translation: "He will stand and shepherd the majesty of Yahweh, in the sovereignty of the name of Yahweh, his God." Here ōz, "strength," is rendered "majesty," and geʾôn, "majesty," is designated as "sovereignty."[19] Hans Walter Wolff deduces a fluid religious-political situation from the identification of ruler with shepherd in the initial metaphor (146). The whole reticulation of paralleled senses is governed here, as it is characteristically in the prophets, by temporal changes and references thereto. So, according to Delbert R. Hillers, the reference of "now" (ʿatah, also "then") is to an immediate future.[20] "Now" is both celebratory and potentially monitory, but the warning drops away (for the moment) when it is matched in antithesis to "the ends of the earth." The earth, not simply a physical entity, parallels those who abide on it. And to abide means to last till the ends of the earth, to avoid the ultimate annihilation built into the word "ends," a poetic compound used always with "earth" from a root that means "coming to nought," "nothing," "cessation," and "extremity." Thus, the end of the thirteen elements of this one verse dovetails with the beginning, and the parallelism provides a constant matching of equivalences, while at the same time the variations create a feeling of adaptive fluidity.

Robert Alter proposes three categories to classify the relations between the first half of a line and the second, namely, "synonymity . . . complementarity (focussing, heightening, intensification, specification) [and] consequentiality," the last being similar, if not identical to what earlier critics called "causal" parallelism.[21] All three of these categories can be correlated with the connections made in this one verse of Micah.

In the verse of the Bible, the sound pattern varies no more pronouncedly than does the sense pattern of the structural parallelism: A two-beat base is often amplified to three; rarely, if ever, more. Or, conversely, a three-beat pattern is syncopated to two. As Benjamin Hrushovski says, "There is an overlapping of several such heterogeneous parallelisms with a mutual reinforcement so that no single element—meaning, syntax, or stress—may be considered as purely dominant or as purely concomitant." Alter adds, "There would seem to be some satisfying feeling of emphasis, for both the speaker and his audience, in stating the same thing twice, with nicely modulated variations." Alter goes on to quote Victor Shklovski: "The perception of disharmony in a harmonious context is important in parallelism."[22] It is well to keep in mind such features, which may be called the ornamental features of parallelism. But we should not limit ourselves before them. After all, they are only surface manifestations on a deep rhythmic and linguistic binder between the prophet and the audience, a binder that admits of an emotional range scored to some degree into the particular pattern of distributing three-beat with two-beat phrases. The scored balances of accentual beats within a verse, according to traditional analysis by Theodore Robinson and others, may evoke particular associations as follows:

2 beats balanced with 2: fear, awe, exuberance (frequent in Psalms)
3 with 2: *qinah*, lamentation (Lamentations)
2 with 3: a sense of well-being (Isa. 40.4)
3 with 3 (very common; includes all of Job)
3 units of 2 beats each in a single hemistich: stocktaking (Pss. 91, 93)[23]

This binder of metrical patterning at one stroke reassures the prophet and the prophet's auditors that the terms are at hand to account for a pressing situation and so there can be repetitions. It also implies that a great wakefulness and effort towards righteousness are called for to compass what comes up in the verses as variation and that the combination of the repetition and the variation taken together will at once threaten the people and inspire them to a perception.

The perception in most poetry is oriented toward the past. Keats, Li Po, and Pindar all offer the profundity of a stocktaking. The poetry of the Hebrew prophet, however, is oriented toward the future. His perception and his intent lead at worst to an informed readiness and at best to a possible restoration but in any case to a future whose features are also compassed in the articulated vision.

Especially in the convention of biblical prophecy, the freedom of parallelism as the basic form of the poetry and the presence of parallelism in "prose" parts of the Old Testament keep the pressure on the utterance to mark itself, as James Kugel demonstrates:

> There is no word for "poetry" in biblical Hebrew. There are a great number of genre classifications in the Bible—words for different types of psalms, hymns, songs and choral arrangements; proverbs, sayings, wordplays; curses, blessings, prayers; histories, tales, genealogies; laws, cultic procedures; speeches, exhortations of moral intent; oracles, predictions, orations of consolation or rebuke—but nowhere is any word used to group individual genres into larger blocs corresponding to "poetry" or "prose." Indeed, where lists of genres exist—as in Proverbs 1.1–6 or Ben Sira (Ecclesiasticus) 47.17—the absence of such groupings comes into bold relief. There is, in fact, no word to describe parallelism per se.[24]

Kugel is making the general point that there is a sort of continuum of heightened expression in which prose may almost duplicate the parallelism of poetry. "There are not two modes of utterance, but many different elements which elevate style and provide for formality and strictness of organization." Citing Proverbs 10.5 as an example, he continues, "The absence of normal signposts heightens attention and sets the discourse off as special and carefully made. . . . parallelism is allied to syntactic simplicity." Consequently, "The extremes of heightened and unheightened speech in the Bible are visible enough. But the 'middle ground' between these extremes is important, and will forever elude a biblical critic equipped only to recognize the maximum of heightening or its total absence."[25]

All of this argument could be extended to a redescription of the religious element in poetry, but that commonplace, unless handled circumspectly, would cut us off quickly from understanding the live properties of the utterance, in the same way that for more than a millennium, despite all the attention given to the subject, learned and devout biblical scholars failed to see that the books of the prophets were mostly written in verse.

Verse, however, these writings are, except where they break into prose—distinctly perceptible when it happens—with various proportions of prose to verse, in Isaiah, Jeremiah, and Ezekiel. Indeed, prose did break into verse on certain occasions before the advent of written prophecy. For what Robinson calls "isolated poems," he lists tribal songs, spells, proverbs, paeans, and dirges.[26] These, however, except for the separate book of Proverbs, could also be called interpolated poems, since they occur on specific occasions, recounted in prose, whose ceremonial character the verse vividly marks. This is the case with Isaac's blessing (Gen. 27.27–29; 49.2–27). Joy and celebration at the crossing of the Red Sea occasion the Song of Moses (Exod. 15.1–18), while Deborah, who is called a prophetess as well as a judge (Judg. 4.4), when her advice and prophecy over the defeat of Sisera is fulfilled, breaks into the long verse run of a song of victory (Judg. 5.1–21). Samson's riddle (Judg. 14.14) and its answer (14.18) are cast in verse to set them off, to signal the special domain their kind of language broaches. Hannah sings her song (1 Sam. 2.1–10) to betoken her thankfulness for Samuel's consecration. David consecrates in song his lament over Saul and Jonathan, linking it prophetically to the condition of Israel (2 Sam. 1.19–27). David's ritual utterances, aside from the legendary ascription to him of many psalms, include a song expressing his thanks for delivery from Saul (2 Sam. 22; Ps. 18). The "last words of David" (2 Sam. 23.1–7) are cast in the form of a succinct prophetic utterance already in the key of later prophecy, though here linked, like the blessing of Isaac, to a formal farewell.

These broader uses indicate that the "literary" prophets from Amos on (writing 760–745 B.C.E.) are exhibiting a specification of function for verse and for their own roles. No longer are kings like David and Saul enlisted as prophets. Prior to Amos, prophets like Elijah and Elisha operated with more direct political force than did their literary successors and with far more magical than poetic effect. Still, their not distant example endows the literary prophets with their political force and even with a touch of their magic.

Zephaniah, who prophesied during the reign of Josiah in Judah (640–609 B.C.E.), dwells simply on the woes to be visited by a foreign invader upon both the Israelites and surrounding peoples. He concludes an initial run with a long *staircase parallelism* about impending doom (Zeph. 1.2–3.7). This form, a sequence of not just two matched statements but of many in a nearly anaphoric series, is well suited to the dire warning. Here the staircase parallelism taken all together stands in "antithetical parallelism" on a large scale to its opposite, the promise of restoration (3.8–20). Nahum vividly details the fall of Nineveh (612 B.C.E.), contrasting it briefly to the correlative restoration of Israel; Habakkuk (writing 608–598 B.C.E.) measures the threatening destruction of the foreign invader against the power and majesty of God. In all these cases, the form of parallelism operates dynamically and can be seen as the underlying organizing principle that repeats itself in order to forge ahead.

The early Amos already exhibits both simplicity and intensity in his utterances, and he may be singled out in his bold outlines to exemplify the activity of the prophet in general. For Amos and the literary prophets, however, God in his distance opens up a possibility of equivalence for Moses' "face to face" confrontation with him by the unremitting pressure of his infinite presence on the forces linking him to prophet and people. Amos turns into an articulate, purified voice that Moses carried through and enacted: "There arose not a prophet since in Israel like unto Moses, whom the Lord knew face to face" (Deut. 34.10). Amos's simplicity can be correlated with the fact, insisted on at the beginning and in the climax of chapter 7, that he was not part of the already traditional dynastic line of prophets, but rather a herdsman—whether a prosperous sheepowner or a simple shepherd. Correlated to the intensity of his utterances is the boldness of his initial movements in crossing from a remote location in the Southern Kingdom of Judah over to the Northern Kingdom of Israel, thereby prophesying for the whole country. Thus, the country if divided in actual political life is united in the imagination, as it were, under threat from the common Assyrian enemy. Amos mentions both Israel and Judah through reference to their kings at the beginning of his prophecy:

The words of Amos, who was among the herdmen of Tekoa, which he saw concerning Israel in the days of Uzziah king of Judah, and in the days of Jeroboam the son of Joash king of Israel, two years before the earthquake. And he said,

The Lord will roar from Zion,
And utter his voice from Jerusalem;
And the habitations of the shepherds shall mourn,
And the top of Carmel shall wither.

(1.1–2)

Not from a prophet's family, Amos is a new man who powerfully inaugurates a new, integral kind of prophecy. Moving from South to North, he is a native Hebrew but also something of a stranger, which suggests that he occupies the formal status of the *ger*, the "resident alien," a regular role in the society.[27] The stranger was a category in a society still nomadic, and the shepherd in this society was somewhat nomadic, too. At the same time, Amos came from a settled village and remained settled when he moved north, thereby also crossing over the categories "settled" and "nomadic." He arrestingly confronts his own supersession of categories when he says, quoting God, "I raised up your sons for prophets" (2.11). Here Amos is both on a par with the hereditary prophets, since he is actually prophesying, and not on a par with them, since he shifts role in this traditional society. He touches base intermittently on the institution, which he joins and transmutes. On the one hand, God "commanded them to prophesy not" (2.11). On the other hand, "Surely the Lord God will do nothing / but he revealeth his secret to the prophets" (3.7).

At the climax of Amos's visions in chapter 7, his prose account leads up to byplay with the king's priest Amaziah when Amos predicts the death of Jeroboam. This priest at once orders Amos out of the country: "O thou seer, go flee thee away into the land of Judah, and there eat bread, and prophesy there: But prophesy not again any more at Beth-el" (7.12–13). This climactic proposed cancellation of the axis prophet-people is countered (and paralleled) by Amos's invocation of his call on the axis God-prophet. He declares under pressure that he was called as a herdsman and is subject to a compelling urgency of utterance:

> And the Lord took me as I followed the flock, and the Lord said unto me, Go, prophesy unto my people Israel. Now therefore hear thou the word of the Lord:
>
> Thou sayest, Prophesy not against Israel,
> And drop not *thy word* against the house of Isaac.
> Therefore thus saith the Lord;
> Thy wife shall be a harlot in the city,
> And thy sons and thy daughters shall fall by the sword,
> And thy land shall be divided by line;
>
> (7.15–17)

Here, in the form of responding quotation, Amos merely expands his message of doom, leading it back to his vision of the plumb line, to which this account is appended. As he said earlier,

> The lion hath roared, who will not fear?
> The Lord God hath spoken, who can but prophesy?
>
> (3.8)

This expression, coupling God and the lion, parallels and spells out the opening couplet of the book, "The Lord will roar from Zion / and utter his voice from Jerusalem" (1.2). Since Jerusalem, indeed, is in the Southern Kingdom and not where Amos stands in the Northern, its centrality is here implicitly conceived of from the beginning as covering the whole of the people in both kingdoms. And God is both majestically hidden and triumphantly manifest, to be read in such portents: "Will a lion roar in the forest when he has no prey?" (3.4).

The shift here into a set of rhetorical questions implies that the processes of decipherable animal activity and the manifestations of God converge in the same pattern of intensifications. The use of the same verb, "roar," *ṣag*, in all three places not only parallels God to a force in the natural terrors of nature. It identifies him with such forces, striking at the outset the note of a fundamental principle in this book, which draws its intensity from an identification of wonders and portents in physical nature with the will of God. Now the God of the Hebrews has been distinguished from the gods of surrounding peoples precisely through a spiritualization of these powers: he is no longer, like the gods of the Assyrians and the Philistines, a god of the sun and moon, of plants and weather. All the more emphatically then does his spiritual power manifest itself when it is declared to comprise those forces, even in the form of simile: "But let judgment run down as waters, / And righteousness as a mighty [*ʿētān*, "ever-flowing," "permanent"] stream" (5.24). In these declarations of intensifying physical nature at the very outset, it is the *habitations* (*nᵊvôt*, "pastures") of the shepherds that mourn, rather than the shepherds themselves, and a bountiful natural expanse that suffers, rather than the cities: "And the top of Carmel shall wither" (1.2). In the "tempest in the day of the whirlwind" (1.14), a metaphorical force is not detachable in its fusions from a physical one. And this holds for the recurrent apocalyptic invocation of fire:

> Thus saith the Lord;
>
> For three transgressions of Judah,
> And for four, I will not turn away *the punishment* thereof;
> Because they have despised the law of the Lord,
> And have not kept his commandments,
> And their lies caused them to err,
> After the which their fathers have walked:
> But I will send a fire upon Judah,
> And it shall devour the palaces of Jerusalem.
>
> (2.4–5)

At the beginning, fire is an element in every oracle: "I will send a fire into the house of Hazael" (1.4), "I will send a fire on the wall of Gaza" (1.7), "I will send a fire on the wall of Tyrus" (1.10), "I will send a fire upon Teman"(1.12), "I will kindle a fire in the wall of Rabbah" (1.14), "I will send a fire upon Moab" (2.2). This fire, found less insistently in Jeremiah and Hosea, will become in the extensions of Amos one of his five visions: "The Lord God called to contend by fire, and it devoured the great deep, and did eat up a part" (7.4). If, earlier in the book, fire is associated just with war, this fire in the great deep goes well beyond human warfare.[28] In an analogue to the destruction of Sodom and Gomorrah, Amos says of Israel, "Ye were as a firebrand plucked out of the burning" (4.11). In the prophesy that Moab shall die with tumult (2.1–9), the military trumpet again enters into fusion with disasters encompassing the natural world, including fire. The same threatens Israel also:

> But seek not Beth-el,
> Nor enter into Gilgal,
> And pass not to Beer-sheba:
> For Gilgal shall surely go into captivity,
> And Beth-el shall come to nought.
> Seek the Lord, and ye shall live;
> Lest he break out like fire in the house of Joseph,
> And devour *it*, and *there be* none to quench *it* in Beth-el.
>
> (5.5–6)

The conventional list of surrounding countries thus builds its repetitions succinctly and pointedly to a culmination in Judah and Israel.

> Thus saith the Lord;
> For three transgressions of Israel,
> And for four, I will not turn away *the punishment* thereof;
> Because they sold the righteous for silver,
> And the poor for a pair of shoes;
> That pant after the dust of the earth on the head of the poor,
> And turn aside the way of the meek:
> And a man and his father will go in unto the same maid,
> To profane my holy name:
> And they lay *themselves* down upon clothes laid to pledge
> By every altar,
> And they drink the wine of the condemned
> *In* the house of their god.
>
> (2:7–8)

The concreteness of Amos's examples gets added force and concision from these paralleled couplings. Selling the righteous for silver provides a common denominator for practices that may include actually selling a compatriot into slavery, violating the "covenant of brother-hood" as happens at Gaza (1.9). Here the sale of the righteous for silver seems both nugatory and greedy by comparison with selling the poor for a pair of shoes, which in this contrastive verse line shows up all the more starkly for the relative triviality of the gain in comparison to the desperation of the act. This focus is expanded, and the parallel ex-tended, in the first hemistich of the next verse, where the poor are op-pressed to the last mite, the dust of the earth, and are turned aside, meek as they are, in a way that makes deflection and oppression ver-sions of each other. This monetary and human injustice is paralleled with an action that elsewhere easily enters into metaphor but here must be taken literally, an access to a prostitution so extreme that it con-founds the generations: "a man and his father will go in unto the same maid." This act is declared to be a profanation on the very name of God. Profanation, in a continued parallel, governs the paired violations of the next verse, acts of intense degradation: using as a cloak at the altar a garment bound through pledge to be returned, and (in Richard S. Scripp's interpretation) partaking of the sacrificial meal with wine instead of water—an ostentation that is hypocritical because the wine had been purchased with money collected as a fine.[29]

In such a confounding, other intensities of violation take place: the Nazarites are induced to break their vow against drinking wine, the prophets forbidden to speak. This ban will oppress the prophet in a vivid image that conflates the agricultural and the prophetic, "pressed . . . as a cart is pressed *that is* full of sheaves." All skill thus vanishes from the swift, from the strong, from the bowman, from the rider, and from the man of courage, who will, in the continuing sharpness of Amos's visualization, "flee away naked":

> And I raised up of your sons for prophets,
> And of your young men for Nazarites.
> *Is it* not even thus, O ye children of Israel?
> Saith the Lord.
> But ye gave the Nazarites wine to drink;
> And commanded the prophets, saying, Prophesy not.
> Behold, I am pressed under you,
> As a cart is pressed *that is* full of sheaves.
> Therefore the flight shall perish from the swift,

And the strong shall not strengthen his force,
Neither shall the mighty deliver himself:
Neither shall he stand that handleth the bow;
And *he that is* swift of foot shall not deliver *himself*:
Neither shall he that rideth the horse deliver himself.
And *he that is* courageous among the mighty
Shall flee away naked in that day,
Saith the Lord.

(2.11–16)

But the power of God, majestic and comprehensive, stands at hand over humankind as it stands over the lights of heaven and the waters of the sea:

Ye who turn judgment to wormwood,
And leave off righteousness in the earth,
Seek him that maketh the seven stars and Orion,
And turneth the shadow of death into the morning,
And maketh the day dark with night:
That calleth for the waters of the sea,
And poureth them out upon the face of the earth:
The Lord *is* his name.

(5.7–8)

As this warning goes on, it returns the people to a cosmic condition reminiscent of the way the universe was before the Creation: "The day of the Lord is darkness and not light" (5.18). In the final resolution and restoration, God's power will be correspondingly comprehensive and congruently extended through the natural world:

Behold, the days come, saith the Lord,
That the plowman shall overtake the reaper,
And the treader of grapes him that soweth seed;
And the mountains shall drop sweet wine,
And all the hills shall melt.
And I will bring again the captivity of my people of Israel,
And they shall build the waste cities, and inhabit *them*;
And they shall plant vineyards, and drink the wine thereof;
They shall also make gardens, and eat the fruit of them.

And I will plant them upon their land,
And they shall no more be pulled up
Out of their land which I have given them,
Saith the Lord thy God.

(9.13–15)

"They will plant . . . and I will plant them." The planting is circular and runs easily from the literal (and spiritually significant) planting of crops by people to the metaphorical planting of people by God. In this metaphor, the prophet reverts to the significant base of the neolithic activity, planting, which complements the one he rose up from, herding. A fullness embracing the natural world is now celebrated: "And the mountains shall drop sweet wine / And all the hills shall melt."

This sharpness of visualization is consistent with the force of the five visions that produces a crescendo in the book. These visions God "showed" Amos, or literally "caused him to see." Midway through the first vision, the plague of locusts, God stops the insects at the prophet's injunction (7.1–3), as he stops midway the fire on the great deep (7.4–6). But the third vision, that of the plumb line to measure the people (7.7–16), will lead on to the death of Jeroboam, and the priest tries to silence the prophet. Thus, the prophet through his visualization actualizes the dynamism of his key role in the transfer of power from God to the people. The fourth vision is wholly metaphorical, hinging on a pun. It is a vision of "summer fruit," *qayiṣ*, and through it, an "end," *qēṣ*, "is come upon my people Israel" (8.1–3). The intensity is totalizing, and the fifth vision, blending into the climax and conclusion of the book, goes to the heart of his prophetic message, dropping ancillary actions and obliquities to center the smitten sanctuary in the collapse of the guilty society:

I saw the Lord standing upon the altar: and he said,
Smite the lintel of the door, that the posts may shake;
And cut them in the head, all of them;
And I will slay the last of them with the sword:
He that fleeth of them shall not flee away,
And he that escapeth of them shall not be delivered.

(9.1)

Amos, like all the prophets after him, rises to concentrations of sense that bring archetypal images here—altar, lintel, posts, head, sword—to bear upon, and to come through, the actual features of a living situation in a specific place and time, broaching a convergence of the temporal and the eternal.

2

"The Burden of the Valley of Vision"

Time and Metaphor in Isaiah

THE ROLE OF the biblical prophet is inseparable from the utterance that at once tries him and guarantees his authenticity. That role in turn is inseparable from his formed response to the interaction between people and God. The prophet is caught in their fate, as they are in his vision of theirs, while all are urged to be aware of God's action upon them in reaction to this whole complex. The prophet is included in their fate; he is one of the people as well as a spokesman for them, as First Isaiah declares:

> For, behold, the Lord, the Lord of hosts,
> Doth take away from Jerusalem and from Judah
> The stay and the staff,
> The whole stay of bread, and the whole stay of water,
> The mighty man, and the man of war,
> The judge, and the prophet,
> And the prudent, and the ancient,
> The captain of fifty, and the honorable man,
> And the counselor, and the cunning artificer, and the eloquent
> orator.

(3.1–3)

The channels are open on the triangle God-prophet-people, and they are so conceived by the prophet: he is open to God's message; he utters it to the people; the people are open to the threat or the promise, the destruction or salvation, at God's hands. The message is always about this, and its signature is its own openness to possibilities and actualities, to fact and apocalyptic definition.

Correspondingly, the metaphors in this prophecy at their fullest can become free-ranging. So, in the passage above, we cannot confine "bread" and "water" simply, even if primarily, to material sustenance. These metaphors are not so much mixed as what is sometimes called absolute, except that even the absolute ones can include a very specific application to a set of life circumstances that at every point is spiritually revealing and spiritually experienced by the prophet. So the message and bearing of the prophet of First Isaiah is at least analogous to and concordant with the notion and image of the Servant brought forward by a prophet of nearly two centuries later, Second Isaiah (Isa. 49–50). The hermeneutic difficulties around the term "Servant," too, occur only when we insist on closing the openness of a metaphor that is sometimes applied to Israel itself, sometimes to a redeemer in the future, but that always has the sense of a proper bearing on the prophet-God or people-God axis or on both. It has been said that the people are the Servant, in the present. The future is certainly open enough in such prophecy, as it has been taken, to include a congruence, typological or not, with the circumstances of Christ's life and death. Not only in the case of the Servant, or the Child-Messiah of Isaiah 51–52, but generally in this and other prophets, the openness of the metaphor renders difficult the application of the prophecy to the sets of specific circumstances that the prophet is certainly addressing simultaneously.

And as are the metaphors, so is the range of theological abstractions—justice, salvation, righteousness, and the like—to which all these strains in Isaiah keep recurring. Brevard S. Childs speaks of the text as sometimes specific and sometimes vague.[1] In Second Isaiah (Isa. 51.4–8, for example), as well as in First, "righteousness," "salvation," "judgment," and "law" come up in an interfusing proximity that makes them hard to distinguish cleanly. And so far as overall emphasis is concerned, the frequent combination in Isaiah of threat and promise, or promise and judgment is puzzling. Such a combination rises out of and reveals the energetic fluidity that the prophet comes forth to utter under an inner pressure, or a fire on the tongue, a pressure he identifies as coming from God.

The prophet delivers his message at a very specific time and under the risk of suffering hostility for the dire possibilities he points to. An essential part of that risk is to enter into the counterstresses of his dire and apocalyptic situation and to continue to give it utterance. It could be said that if the situation were clear, his utterance would not be needed. So he presents judgment and salvation, suffering servants, and global terms for whole peoples who are both rejected and assimilated. They, like the Israelites, may be personified as fields or wives or vineyards and, at the same time, as possessors of fields and wives and vineyards that will prosper or languish accordingly as they respond. The "invective-threat," Hermann Gunkel's *Scheltrede-Drohwort*, carries the burden of this pressure. And as Childs says, "Gunkel's thesis of a prophetic liturgy was able for the first time to take account of the great variety of literary forms within the one oracle (woe oracle, national lament, prophetic oracle, Torah liturgy) and to establish the function of the oracle within the cultic life of the people."[2] However, the form-critical definitions have, along with the advantage of finding terms for strands of utterance, the disadvantage of suggesting that the text is atomized rather than remarkable for bringing all these modes of discourse together and for leaving the individual forms behind insofar as the prophet's utterance is apprehended as a unified one. And types of song found in other biblical contexts are also conflated into prophecy: tribal song (Gen. 4.23); spells (Gen. 9.25; 27.39); proverb comparisons, *mešhalim* (Proverbs and elsewhere); paean (Exod. 15.1–18o; Judg. 50); lamentation, *qinah* (Psalms; Deut. 32.1–43).

Religion for Isaiah and other prophets is at once a context and a focusing subject, one which links a whole people to a Supreme Being. This religion defines politics in a way so constantly changing in its dynamism that even a term like "theocratic" would be somewhat misleading. And of course, so far as the cultic life of the people, their relation to God, is concerned, we know that cultic life only through the prophet, and it can never be separated from the other vectors, prophet-God and people-prophet. In the triangle of forces envisioned by the Hebrew prophet, the side of the speaker determines what the side of the people will mean (and the other way around), while both are determined not just by the presence but by the action and the reaction of Jehovah. In the theological situation, which is also a political and a dialogic one, the poetry is founded on a life-and-death urgency that also enters into repetition of its central subject, repetition of the dire threat against the people from invaders, of their dire need and a possible transcendence of it, of the omnipotent and potentially dire vigilance of God. Repetition, in the form of thought-rhyme or parallelism, is the defining form of the utterance as well. Its semantic and rhythmic base can thus be taken as an echo of its context and content. Yet, the set posture of the prophet about to speak brings him under the pressure of his utterance into a speech that finds fulfillment as it presses beyond the formal and logical antitheses he codes into his poetic lines. He carries his utterance forward into overriding hopefulness, or (in the mode of Jeremiah) into nearly overmastering grimness. The canonizers, in the scantness of their historical information, mistakenly saw Isaiah as one person, but the book Isaiah brings together prophets whose emphases are associable, and now commentators are again unifying it as a later redaction aimed to bring the separate units together.

Within a single verse and within runs of verse, the thought-rhyme of obligatory dual statement in parallelism can match the first of its repeatable elements to the second and to others on a range that is fairly free. Along the lines of Bishop Lowth's pioneering analysis, there are a number of parallelisms: synonymous, antithetic, formal, emblematic in idea or through simile, stairlike, and introverted.[3] In all the prophets, there is a limited stock of themes to which they return and that they recombine so pervasively that almost any utterance can be taken as parallel by echo, partial or whole, or by antithesis, partial or whole, to any other.

These themes are, in a sense, preexisting attitudes conditioned by a political present towards which the prophet is expected to take a God-centered future orientation. The pattern type of a "tribal" society that first differentiates a priest-king from the group and then splits those leadership functions would find echoes in every society's assignment of roles to a poet, even the modern one. Shelley's jejune notion of poets as the "unacknowledged legislators of mankind" would thus find a complex grounding in social practice, where for "unacknowledged," one would read "skewed" or "conflated." And it is not just the priestly function that the poet fulfills, though it is mainly that. Saul was a king so little known as a prophet that his role as one must be asserted.[4] David and Solomon were differently accorded a poetic function along with the kingly one. Modern society, of course, splits its functions into far more categories than those that obtained in ancient Israel; we should attend to the consequences of the fact that Isaiah, from the modern point of view, combined the functions of editorial writer, theologian, seer, public orator, and royal adviser, along with that of poet.

In Isaiah, there is a frequent adduction of social structures like buying and selling, marrying, and even redeeming and judging in legal contexts, that are transformed when one of the parties, as the prophet sets it up, is the God who transcends such conditions. At the other extreme, the formula "as nothing" comes up along this axis, as the prophecy envisages the incomparability of God:

> All nations before him *are* as nothing;
> And they are counted to him less than nothing, and vanity.
> To whom then will ye liken God?
> Or what likeness will ye compare unto him?
>
> (40.17–18)

But God cannot be collapsed, nor can the people wholly be contained, within their single existence. They are inescapably involved in the dynamism of forces.

Part of the prophet's reaction moves dynamically along another vector of the triangle, the side that connects the prophet to God; God inspires the prophet, and the prophet responds to this call. And all these actions bear on what lies before us as readers of the prophet who, as such, are in the position of the people hearing. He "pours forth," or "proclaims"—in the verb that his designation derives from, *nāvʾi*, *nāvā*—under the direct authority of God, "The Lord Jehovah *is* my strength and *my* song" (12.2).

Through this process the prophet has a vision connected to his burden, "The burden [or "oracle"] that Isaiah the son of Amoz did see [literally, "visioned," ul *ḥazah*]" (13.1). False prophets, on the other hand, have no light: "If they speak according to this word [or "thing"] it is because there is no light in them [literally, "in it," *dāvār ha zeh ašer ʾēn lô šaḥar*]" (8.20). And what the prophet proclaims entails a dire risk that differentiates him from poets in comparable traditions. He undertakes the danger of exposing himself to telling the people what by definition they do not want to hear; he recalls them to what the consequences are on their side of the triangle, the relation between people and God, as it derives from both specific and long-range political events.

The prophet in Israel drew not just on personal charisma—to use the terms that Max Weber applied to this society[5]—but on the expectation of having a charismatic function to fulfill by virtue of personal exposure as a channel of a divine message. That exposure carried with it the dangers of stress, exhibited variously by Hosea and Jeremiah, among others. And it also carried the danger of invalidation: there were such things as false prophets, and at any time the charisma of a true prophet could be threatened and the prophet be maltreated by being accounted a false one.[6]

In neither Homeric nor Vedic society was the poet exposed to the danger faced by the Hebrew prophet. Homer's utterance began under the precondition not of risk but of validated security. The risk of the Hebrew prophet, by contrast, is exemplified by a contemporary of Jeremiah who was put to death for uttering prophecies having substantially the same message as his. Jeremiah lived much of his life under extreme risk: he was put in stocks, condemned to death, imprisoned, thrown down a cistern, and exiled for life, against his will, to Egypt.

In the open utterance of all these counterstresses, the prophecy is locutionary, perlocutionary, and illocutionary, all at once. It states, and in its verse form it repeats, series of capital propositions. These capital propositions are stated to "open the eyes and ears" of the hearers, and so are perlocutionary.[7] And they are also meant to induce a reactive change; they are illocutionary. In the rhetorical frameworks we take for granted, the political speech, the sermon, and the poem are fused; and fused with the permanence that soon canonized these utterances as parts of the Bible, putting the books of the prophets on a par with the Law and the Writings.

In any poetry, and in fact in any written utterance, that self-nesting, reactive set of presuppositions that Paul Grice identifies is suspended, along with much else.[8] The conversational exchange is sublated; with that is sublated the dominance of the "symbolic," in Jacques Lacan's sense, that obtains in any human converse, especially as this structure is revealed in the parallel situation of the psychiatric interview. The listening analyst is silent, which gives the patient access to his or her own structurings of the symbolic. In literature, however, this situation is reversed: it is the speaker who offers and structures the symbolic, and the listener takes this in, while reacting in ways that do engage the psyche. But to inspect that psyche is a diversion, because the action is coded into the utterance itself and retrieving it involves a hermeneutic attention, one way or another, to its own structures. When the utterance is a scripture, it asserts its finality, whether or not some other auditor than the one for whom it is intended assents to that finality. When it is a poem, it has built into it the cues that restructure it by a repetition incremental to its ongoing discourse. This distinction, between poetry and what amounts to conversational prose, supersedes the distinction between oral and written. That is, the difference between conversation, or oratory, and any kind of verse is far greater than the difference between written and oral. And in any kind of literature, the auditors trade their silence for access to a message whose special properties have been highlighted because the speaker has induced a special code.[9]

Biblical parallelism in the hands of Isaiah offers a verse that masters its urgency by a corresponding dynamic fluidity. The possibility of parallelism controls that dynamic fluidity, without locking into the actuality of fixed members, as Second Isaiah shows:

2   Look unto Abraham your father,
And unto Sarah *that* bare you:
For I called him alone,
And blessed him, and increased him.
3   For the Lord shall comfort Zion
He will comfort all her waste places;
And he will make her wilderness like Eden,
And her desert like the garden of the Lord;
Joy and gladness shall be found therein,
Thanksgiving, and the voice of melody.
4   Hearken unto me, my people;
And give ear unto me, O my nation:
For a law shall proceed from me,
And I will make my judgment to rest for a light of the people.
My righteousness *is* near;
5   My salvation is gone forth,
And mine arms shall judge the people;

The isles shall wait upon me,
And on mine arm shall they trust.
6   Lift up your eyes to the heavens
And look upon the earth beneath:
For the heavens shall vanish away like smoke
And the earth shall wax old like a garment,
And they that dwell therein shall die in like manner:
But my salvation shall be for ever,
And my righteousness shall not be abolished.
7   Hearken unto me, ye that know righteousness,
The people in whose heart *is* my law;
Fear ye not the reproach of men,
Neither be ye afraid of their revilings.
8   For the moth shall eat them up like a garment,
And the worm shall eat them like wool:
But my righteousness shall be for ever,
And my salvation from generation to generation.
9   Awake, awake, put on strength,
O arm of the Lord;
Awake, as in the ancient days,
In the generations of old.

(51.2–9)

These texts sweep through the whole of biblical history, since the whole sacred past of the people is counted as having a moral bearing on the present. In this case, the present involves the imminent release from Babylonian captivity around 536 B.C.E., through the agency of the Persian conquest of Babylon under Cyrus. Once Avram, upright father, had been called Avraham, father of multitudes (in Genesis), then the multitudes will be associable to him forever. The recollection is made by the prophet not only by invoking the name of both father and mother. In verse 3, the mother's barrenness is hinted at, if not wholly paralleled, in the "desert" that precedes the "garden," which God is called on to show that he will create anew. Abraham's new name is also hinted at in the very verb of "increase," *rāvāh*, "Av-raham." And the verb is emphasized by calling the increase a blessing through the coupling of parallelism, "blessed him / and increased him," as well as by the near rhyme of the two verbs, *ʾavarkēhû ve ʾarbēhû*. Such a vast backward leap, in the invoked perspective of God, includes a forward leap to the prosperity of a future that, in the light of Third Isaiah, will include even more multitudes than just the Israelites. This future look, "he will make her wilderness like Eden," entails an even further backward look, to the beginning in Eden. But it is not said that Eden will be recaptured; it is presented in the form first of a simile and then in the intensification of the succeeding parallel assertion, like "the garden of the Lord," a term that is less precise, though equally historicized, if read as a synonym for Eden. The activities of the restored Israelites, it may be said, will become parallel to Eden, even if it is impossible for them to become fully Edenic. Indeed, what guarantees the possibility is not only the long fidelity to the father Abraham through history but, situationally, the resemblance of their flight from Mesopotamia to his own long before.[10]

Time is evoked as overriding past and future in the verb schemes here, a situation that some would attribute to the division of Hebrew tenses, not formally into pasts, presents, and futures, but rather into perfectives (usually read as past) and imperfectives (usually read as future). In addition to the omnipresent possibility of the seemingly illogical reversal of these tenses in the "*vāv* consecutive," which means that under certain conditions the imperfective is reversed into a past, or the perfective into a future, there is also a "prophetic perfect" (*perfectum propheticum*), which reads past or present as though it were a future. And the turn in these verses around "shall comfort" and "will comfort"—with an exact repetition of the same verb rather than the normal partial synonym or antonym of parallelism—is actually given in the perfective, *niḥam*, literally, "comforts," or even, "has comforted." The verb offers what has to be construed as a future in the grammar of a present or a past. Commenting specifically on Ezekiel 37.12, "I will open your graves and cause you to come up out of your graves and bring you into the land of Israel," André Lamorte says of the prophetic perfect generally, "The verbs are perfects. . . . Their translation by a present is imposed by the viewpoint of the prophet who sees (in spirit) the opening of tombs and the return to the reviving country."[11]

The prose of the call in Isaiah 6 moves into a timeless revelation in its evocation of seraphim, though it is keyed to a precise time, the year of the death of Uzziah, 739 B.C.E. The sign of Immanuel is a sign for the

future (7.13–14). It is soon matched by a sign from the remote, apocalyptic past: "Lucifer, son of the morning, How art thou fallen from
heaven" (14.12). For an alien people, in the "Burden of Dumah," time
is leveled to indiscriminateness in the reply to "Watchman, what of the
night?" "The morning cometh, and also the night: / . . . Return, come"
(21.11–12). This long view of Isaiah conflates Exodus and the Assyrian
invasion, "My people went down aforetime in Egypt to sojourn there;
and the Assyrian oppressed them without cause" (52.4).

The prophet, touching base in his deployment of verb tenses on the
prophetic perfect, sees the event as already having happened in the future. The only reference in First Isaiah to exile is a stark causal-factual
statement, "Therefore my people is exiled," *lakēn gālāh ammî* (5.13).
Here, stating the future as already having happened energizes the prophetic perfect. This grammatical hinge is consonant not only with
shifts in time and with a fluidity of metaphor but also with transpositions into varieties of perspectives on time, transpositions that entail a
range of reference, with or without a shift of metaphor, to the specific,
dynamic relation between people and God. In a sense, since the prophetic perfect can refer to the present or to the past as well as to the
future, it already projects the fluidity of metaphor onto a time line. We
do not feel that the application of Abraham or Eden or Zion, as they are
used here, or of Exodus, as it is frequently used in Isaiah (4.5; 11.15;
30.1–6; 43; 48.21), is different in metaphorical structure from the application of figures lacking a temporal structure like river and desert,
vineyard, and so on. When, in 55.3, two eras of time are fused through
the Covenant's identification with David (as in Isa. 1.26), the freedom
of association and of metaphor formation prevents the time implication
of these typologies from hardening into figures. And the Flood is an
analogue as well as a historical event in 54.9: "like the waters of Noah."
Jacob is invoked, partly as ancestor and partly for his name "Israel" in
42.24: "Who gave Jacob for a spoil, / And Israel to the robbers?" There
is a constant recourse to sweeping assertions over a vast stretch of time:
"And I will restore thy judges as at the first, / And thy counsellors as
at the beginning" (1.26). This verse echoes the opening of Genesis and
overlaps the whole time process, even if the immediate reference leads
back to the Book of Judges. God is said to press the prophet towards the
long view of time:

Then said I, Lord, how long? And he answered,
Until the cities be wasted without inhabitant,
And the houses without man,
And the land be utterly desolate,
And the Lord have removed men far away,
And *there be* a great forsaking in the midst of the land.

(6.11–12)

"And it shall come to pass at the end of days," *vehāyāh be'aḥarît ha yōmîm* (2.2), presents an even sweep into the future.

In the lines quoted earlier (51.2–9), there is a linear time span from Eden into the proximate restored future that the verb tenses turn into something like a cyclical, and then a spiraling, time. There is the horizon of eternity always in view when God is in question: "my salvation shall be for ever" (51.6), "my righteousness shall be for ever" (51.8); "for ever" translating *le'ôlām* in both instances, an expression commonly found as a terminal asseveration in Psalms and elsewhere. There is the long, residually dynastic view, "my salvation from generation to generation" (51.8), the phrase having the ritual emphasis of frequent recurrence, as again is often found in Psalms. Then there is the further perspective of the phrase translated "as in the ancient days," *kîme qedem*. Hebrew *yôm*, "day," refers not just to a twenty-four-hour cycle but to any period of time. Moreover, *qedem*, "ancient," or "formerly," literally means "east," and so the term visualizes time in a light that converges with space—as is also done with Eden, making this term strike the note of parallelism with the Eden mentioned seven verses before. This phrase is here paralleled to "the generations of old," *dôrôt 'ôlāmîm*, where *dôrôt*, "generations," conflates the phrase "from generation to generation" into a single instance of the "generation to generation," *le dôr dôrîm*, in the previous verse, linking it still more closely to eternity, since the term translated of old, *'ôlāmîm*, is a variant of *'ôlām*, the "eternity" of verse 8.

Even in these verses, there is no single view of time, but it would be rash to infer a confusion about time. Rather, there is a continuous opening of perspectives. The provisionality of one view, like the provisionality of the one historical point at which the Israelites find themselves or the provisionality of the particular definition that might be accorded their moral situation, finds qualification and validation rather than cancellation in the divine view towards which the prophet is stretching and inducing his auditors to stretch. And there are further angles on time in Isaiah: a frequent reference to the "moment," *rega͑*, a unit so small that it could be translated as "flash," or "twinkling," and that is characterized as a "small moment," *rega͑ qatôn*, in 54.7: "For a small moment have I forsaken thee." This reassurance is picked up in the next verse: "I hid my face from thee for a moment." In this context, the moment is at once countered by its opposite: "But with everlasting kindness will I have mercy on thee" (54.8); the term for "everlasting" again being *ôlām*.[12] There is the related, perhaps more intensive, notion of the "instant," *feta͑*, such as in 29.5: "it shall be at an instant, suddenly," *feta͑ pit͑ôm*. The proximate future is also seen as a short span in 29.17: "a little while," *ôd meaṭ*. This is picked up, made present, and varied in 29. 22: "now," *͑atāh*, a locution given twice. Two things are brought about in the flash of a *rega͑* in 47.9: "these two things shall come to thee in a moment," and the two things are dire.

In chapter 18, the Nubian Kingdom, as well as being distant in space, is set against the Assyrian, and the contrast offers a somewhat different time structure, since the Assyrian is seen as never coming to fruition, "like a cloud of dew in the heat of harvest" (18.4). "It shall come to pass in that day" is a formula invoked in 27.13. Another is the formula of 2.2: "in the end of days," *be͗aḥarît hayômîm*. The application of Exodus in Isaiah, such as in 11.15, projects the remote past forward. The force of the echo of Exodus carries into the future: "And the Lord will create upon every dwelling place of mount Zion . . . a cloud and smoke by day, and the shining of a flaming fire by night" (4.5). The repetition here implies a glorification connected to a separation, coupling judgment and destruction. If the collocation of Israel and Egypt in 30.1–6 is taken as referring to a recent or proximate time, it constitutes at once a variation on the analogy to Exodus and a reversion of sorts to conditions closer to hand.

Then there is the more indefinite future, unrealized because Israel will not hearken: "Who will listen to the time to come [*le͗aḥôr*]?" (42.23). In 56.12, a brighter future of indefinite extent is envisaged: "Tomorrow shall be as this day / And much more abundant." The "acceptable time," *ᶜet raṣôn* (49.8), is still another notion hard to coordinate with all these others, if the goal of coordination were not manifestly against the spirit of the time ranges in Isaiah and in other prophets, too. "Declaring the end from the beginning" (46.10) at once suggests a complete cycle and reverses the ultimate future into the ultimate past, a millennial transfer related to the assertion of 48.7: "They are created now, and not from the beginning; / Even before the day when thou heardest them not." The sequence of 44.24–25 envisages a confounding of space, time, thought, and condition through the agency of an omnipotent God clear on all these aspectual changes: "I *am* the Lord . . . / That turneth wise men backward."

"Thou shalt take up this proverb [*mašal*] against the king of Babylon" (14.4). And the "likeness," the meaning that is also nested in *mašal*, may lead to a dissolution into identity, as the nations are imagined to say to Israel, "Art thou become like [*nimšaltah*] unto us?" (14.10). While God is spoken of as sending a message, he is also characterized as exceeding the understanding that might derive from the use of metaphoric comparison: "*There is* no searching of his understanding" (40.28). "To whom then will ye liken God? / Of what likeness will ye compare unto him?" (40.18).

> *It is* he that sitteth upon the circle of the earth,
> And the inhabitants thereof *are* as grasshoppers;
> That stretcheth out the heavens as a curtain,
> And spreadeth them out as a tent to dwell in:
> That bringeth the princes to nothing;
> He maketh the judges of the earth as vanity.
>
> (40.22–23)

The fluidity of time-conceptions and the fluidity of metaphoric usage are here interdependent, notably in the passages quoted above where the figurative language condenses images of catastrophe with images of swiftness. "The heavens shall vanish away like smoke" (51.6)—whether or not "vanish away" should really read "be scattered"—remarkably suggests both lingering and speed, since this is the way smoke disappears: it will hang around for hours, but tomorrow it is gone. And this is the way that not just the conditions for the Israelites will disappear but so also will the firmament where, they presumed, God would be steady. Connected with this is an image of vagueness: smoke is uniform in its gaseous state. It is as difficult to see through smoke as it is for a corrupt people to see God aright (and images of seeing abound in Isaiah)—or to see him without the aid of a prophet. The primitive notion of a God who recreates the cosmos need not be invoked here, any more than we need apply the notion of the aftermath of a universal conflagration. But neither can these templates of mythical thinking be dismissed. In the next passage, the prophet moves towards comparable conceptions:

> *Art* thou not it that hath cut Rahab,
> *And* wounded the dragon?
> *Art* thou not it which hath dried the sea,
> The waters of the great deep?

(51.9–10)

In any case, the instantaneous but somewhat dilatory destruction of the heavens takes place in a different time frame from that of the earth that shall "wax old like a garment" (51.6). Both the garment and the smoke are similes in which the *tenor* and the *vehicle* are firm. The later simile, comparing persons instead of the earth to a garment, is less firm—"the moth shall eat them up like a garment" (51.8)—especially if the modern translation, "worm," instead of "moth," is read. Then the literal becomes vivid: worms eat the dead as moths eat garments; the eating is literal, the garment figurative. The structure of the figure shifts again in the parallel complement of this line, "the worm shall eat them like wool," where, once more, all three of the members, worm, eat, and wool, can be taken literally, if taken separately, but not if they are taken together. Normal barriers are to be confounded in experience as they are in the language here. And the remedy exists in the figure shortly to come, "Awake, awake, put on strength" (51.9), since the word for "put on," *livši*, is from *lavaš*, "to clothe," a semantic sibling of "garment."[13] At this point, clothing is wholly figurative but strength is literal, while the term "awake" spans both literal and figurative as it rings one of several converging tonic notes in the prophet's utterance. The "arm of the Lord," too, is a dead metaphor, livened in this context by the body references of the preceding figures. Contradictions can nest the more powerfully in the breadth of figurative utterance: "For though thy people Israel be as the sand of the sea, / Yet a remnant of them shall return" (10.22). Or again, the process can fuse the singing of the people and the prophet with the "singing" of nature:

> The whole earth is at rest *and* is quiet
> They break forth singing.
> Yea the fir trees rejoice at thee.
>
> (14.7–8)

And the breaking forth into song, *poṣḥû rinnāh*, is perhaps not a dead metaphor, because the verb meaning "to break," or "to crush," still emphasizes the utterance that is akin to the natural processes soon mentioned. Where Tyre sings as a harlot (23.16), the oracle of Jerusalem comes forth as "the burden of the valley of vision" (22.1), claiming, "From the uttermost part of the earth have we heard songs" (24.16). In the increasing specification and amplification of metaphor, fat abundance is turned around to destruction (25.6). To "swallow death in victory" (25.8) introduces another apocalyptic note, a third turn, after the first of prosperity and the second of adversity, that perhaps offers traces of a primitive engulfing deity. "Salvation will God appoint *for* walls and bulwarks" (26.1) builds the spiritual and the physical together in still another dimension, as does "We wait for light and behold darkness" (9.1–4).

Relations among time predictions and metaphors come forward to expand and intricate. The fate of Judah repeats the fate of Israel. But their people will be recovered out of the many foreign lands named in 1.11–16. From chapters 13 through 23, those lands will be assigned their own fates in cogent images. Yet, of the Rod of Jesse, "he shall not judge after the sight of his eyes" (11.3). But then this turmoil turns at once to a dire outcome: "Their eye shall not spare children" (13.18).

The fertility imagery of the agricultural cycle, widespread in the prophets, cannot easily be assigned a merely figural structure since, in the primitive association patterns studied by James G. Frazer and others, physical health, spiritual health, prosperity, human fertility, and

the orderly succession of good crops from abundant water all belong together. Hence, these terms cannot be assigned fixed roles in the propositions of a metaphoric deep structure. In 4.5, there is a switch to the
analogy between a vine crop and a woman, and the notion of the
woman and her faithful fertility is much used in the prophets, as it is
in chapters 9 and 10 here. Combining the vine and the fertile woman
raises the question of figuration to the second degree, since either term,
taken by itself, would be a complete figure. In 54.2–5, the wife and the
desolate women are at once separated and associated. "The spoiling of
the daughter of my people," šod bat ʿamî (22.4), a phrase attributed to
God by and through the prophet, again condenses the historical process
via this metaphor.

"The grass faileth" (15.6) sounds the alarm of a disruption in the
reliable time of the annual cycle of growing. This image easily accords
with the common fertility figures. But the figure of grass later intensifies in the assertion that "All flesh is grass" (40.6), a direct metaphor
with a different structure but the same purport (though less ominous
than the images of the body as a garment or as wool). Within this pattern, various intensifications are broached by the prophet: "A man shall
be . . . as rivers of water in a dry place "(32.2). Suddenly, a human abundance multiplies with more force, since the word here for "river," feleg,
also means "channel" and comes from a root meaning "split," "di-
vide." When it is said that "the desert shall rejoice, and blossom as the
rose" (35.1), in this context a flower (not grapes or grain), something
rare and delicate, helps the very desert join in the jubilation usually
accorded men rather than plants. "I will open rivers in high places"
(41.18) combines mountains and rivers, two loci of rich association in
a geographical enigma that has no recourse to figure. In 55.10, it is snow
that causes fertility, a nonfigural but arresting deduction that is easily
followed and carried through to the powerful comparison, in the next
verse, of this natural process to the speech and edict of God, "So shall
the word be that goeth forth out of my mouth," and culminating in
the image "the myrtle tree . . . shall be . . . an everlasting sign" (55.13).
Without such controls, "Their molten images *are* wind and confusion"
(4.29), and what is solid, if handled idolatrously, disappears in a bewil-
dering emptiness.

The injunction "Enter into the rock" (2.10) offers the opposite of an expansive centering. This rock is not the refuge or defense of Psalms, as the continuation makes clear:

> And the Lord alone shall be exalted in that day.
> And the idols he shall utterly abolish.
> And they shall go into the holes of the rocks,
> And into the caves of the earth,
> For fear of the Lord. . . .
> In that day a man shall cast
> His idols of silver, and his idols of gold,
> Which they made *each one* for himself to worship,
> To the moles and to the bats;
> To go into the clefts of the rocks,
> And into the tops of the ragged rocks, . . .
>
> (2.17–21)

The light of day connects to the light of the eyes, physical and spiritual, and recursively at all points to the "vision," *hazah*, of the prophet across time into the future: "Arise, shine, for thy light is come, / And the glory of the Lord is risen upon thee" (60.1). "Then shall thy light break forth as the morning" (58.8) connects the body to the cosmos and soon after, in 58.10, the prophet envisions dawn in darkness. In 58.11–12, the vision undergoes easy and paralleling transitions to images of a garden, of water and springs, and then to the conception of rebuilding the waste in an eternal time span. "To provoke the eyes of his glory" (3.8) is the early, condensed image of the effect of human iniquity on divine vision.

These passages and many others like them provide good examples both of the reticulation of metaphors and of their free transposition. In the run of chapters 16–20, fire, briers, forest, and trees are imaged in both literal and metaphorical senses that converge in the reach of the utterance. Since both a figure and its specific constituents may be parallel to one another in form, in content, or in spiritual reference, the freedom of metaphor makes parallelism all the more simply a loose connector, neither more nor less definitively enclosing than the two- or three-beat measure of the randomly progressive rhythms. In such freedom, First Isaiah can proceed immediately to a final vision, resting on images that hover between the literal and the figurative:

> And it shall come to pass in the last days,
> *That* the mountain of the Lord's house shall be established in the top of the mountains,
> And shall be exalted above the hills;
> And all nations shall flow into it.
>
> (2.2)

Just before this passage, a spiritual anguish is made comprehensive through the image of the trees that exemplify the fertility cycle and the prosperity and joy connected with it but also the idolatry of neighboring peoples to whom the Israelites sometimes yielded: "For they shall be ashamed of the oaks [terebinths] which ye have desired" (1.29). The range provides for a further yoking of large categories. In 12.3, there is a coupling of strength and song; and in 16.11, other categories: "My *bowels* sound like a *harp* for *Moab*" (my italics). There is a still more intense melding of categories, but again without a special, underlying, and mapable figural structure, in 34.3–4:

> And the mountains shall be melted with their blood.
> And all the host of heaven shall be dissolved,
> And the heavens shall be rolled together like a scroll [*sēpher*].

(The "book," *sēpher*, is picked up again in verse 16, when it is identified with God.) In what may really be a final statement, at the conclusion of chapter 59, the conjunctions are so forceful that it is impossible simply either to assert or to deny the presence of metaphor:

> And my words which I have put in thy mouth,
> Shall not depart out of thy mouth,
> Nor out of the mouth of thy seed,
> Nor out of the mouth of thy seed's seed, saith the Lord,
> From henceforth and forever.
>
> (59.21)

The speaking God converges here with the speaking prophet who, in any case, is his mouthpiece for these words; and over time, this utterance becomes identified with the people, or that part of them that can be reckoned in a presumably spiritual line of descent from the prophet (in which case, "seed" is a metaphor): "Nor out of the mouth of thy seed's seed." The long-range view of time, constantly modulated in all three of the prophets who are grouped as Isaiah, brings the sense of the utterance and the subject of the utterance into one intense formulation.

3

Exemplary Intensities in Jeremiah

J EREMIAH KNOTS HIS utterances about God's warnings through a presentation of his own person. His text at times tenses to bursts of
recursive image; at other times, it slackens to episodes of autobiographical narrative. The signification of the episodes ranges from the schematically allegorical to the illustratively self-explanatory. In the given
context and through the shift of rhythm and focus, the prophet's ges-
tures plait the actual and the figural, the word and the thing (the Hebrew term *davar* means both) into a many-dimensioned communication,
in which the prophet is both a passive sufferer at God's hands through
the people and an active communicator of God's message to the people.

The register of Isaiah, to which the prophets who wrote or were
collected under that name recur, involves a long-range vision, whether
of the fall of the Northern Kingdom to the Assyrians in 721 B.C.E.,
imminent in the writings of First Isaiah from 739 on; or the exile in
Babylon after the final sack of Jerusalem in 587, the end of which is envisaged as imminent by Second Isaiah, once the successes of the even-
handed Persians from 549 on promise a return; or the messianic hopes
of the Third Isaiah at some time after the release in 539 and the recon-
struction of the Temple in 515. The long-range vision subsumes the particular emphases residing in the First Isaiah's warnings of the necessity
for a proper bearing toward God under the pressure of the Assyrians;
the less political injunctions of Second Isaiah towards endurance and
hope; and Third Isaiah's eschatalogical sweep.

The register of the single prophet Jeremiah involves a shorter range
and still greater concentration, because through the forty years of his
activity, from the call in 627 to the final fall of Jerusalem, he wrote under
pressure of responding to and formulating a politics and theology of
desperation under increasingly dire events. In the triangle of forces—
God, people, prophet—all the vectors are compacted so as to adapt to

a situation that, in the near but foreseeable future (visible only to the prophet), is hopeless. These concentrations are mounted and proclaimed as necessary to express a perception of the hopelessness.

In Jeremiah, the poetry itself coils its senses out of the drama of the prophet's life.[1] Framing these verse utterances, he expands on the events he suffered through in a narrative prose or proselike discourse that will be given a still fuller rhythmic role in Ezekiel, Zechariah, and Daniel.

For Isaiah, much of the drama bears on the moment of his call: six-winged seraphim come, the room fills with smoke, and God touches a burning coal to his mouth (Isa. 6). Jeremiah will have much to live through, but his actual call is presented more simply, in what would seem to be the same tradition: God touches Jeremiah directly on the mouth (Jer. 1.9). Then his prophecy persists, internalized and burning, kindling the dialogue—here frequently cast in dramatic interchanges—between God and prophet, in such a way as to consume the people: "Behold, I will make my words in thy mouth fire, / And this people wood, and it shall devour them" (5.14). Jeremiah's whole life is implicated in the prophetic process, as he keeps emphasizing. For Jeremiah, God is an ongoing, internal fire, interacting with his anguish over his call:

> Then I said, I will not make mention of him,
> Nor speak any more in his name.
> But *his word* was in mine heart as a burning fire
> Shut up in my bones.

> (20.9)

This intensifies his situation beyond the situation of Isaiah and interiorizes the prophetic function not just as a set discourse but as a whole responsive way of being that registers deeply and painfully in the body, both in what is enacted upon the prophet and how he responds. So he registers in his very body the sway of the false prophets:

> Mine heart within me is broken
> Because of the prophets;
> All my bones shake.

> (23.9)

Jeremiah, calling himself a *naᶜar*, "child" (1.6), echoes and turns round the verses of God's speech in 1.5 that tell how God had consecrated him in the womb:

Before I formed thee in the belly I knew thee;
And before thou camest forth out of the womb I sanctified thee;
And I ordained thee a prophet unto the nations.

Images and themes persist, carrying the regular Hebrew parallelism of individual verses on to overriding recursions through it. Giving birth, with all its promise and danger, and with what Jeremiah presents powerfully as its pain and frustration, plays across his whole text. Very soon this term "child," *naᶜar*, is transposed into the "childhood," or "youth," *neᶜûrayik*, of the whole Hebrew people:

Go and cry in the ears of Jerusalem, saying, Thus saith the
    Lord;
I remember thee, the kindness of thy youth,
The love of thine espousals.

                                                                      (2.2)

The term "kindness of thy youth," *ḥesed neᶜûrayik*, picks up *naᶜar* from 1.6 and makes it positive as it is applied to the whole people. Indeed, the people, in the mind of God and the mouth of the prophet, merge in the powerful word *ḥesed*, "kindness," or "loving-kindness," since that untranslatable term encapsulates both God's holy beneficence towards the people and theirs toward him. The two-way relation makes them holy ones, *ḥasidim*—or it would, if they were not falling away from the ideal relationship of the Exodus recalled in the subsequent verses. Such thematic threads act through the whole text as superfixes on the parallelism of the individual verses. The child throughout is implicated in the pressures of long-range time.

Weep ye not for the dead, neither bemoan him:
But weep sore for him that goeth away:
For he shall return no more,
Nor see his native country.

                                                                    (22.10)

This formulation is again resumptive; by implication, at this point it posits a time that allows for no regeneration. The literal statement, "And he will [not] see the country of his birth [*môladetô*]," echoes and transposes, in the frequent long-range parallelism, Jeremiah's wish that having been conceived he never come to birth (20.17). A logic of seemingly random but cumulative compression works—as in staircase parallelism—through the summaries of all these events. The inscrutability of time and the hardness of Israel's sufferings turn out to yield the surprise of sudden reversal: the people will "flee . . . out of Babylon" (50.20). Babylon, too, suffers the vent of this dire transformation. It will now be "burnt" and "desolate." Babylon's mountain is no Zion; it is now destroyed:

> Behold, I *am* against thee, O destroying mountain,
> Saith the Lord,
> Which destroyest all the earth;
> And I will stretch out mine hand upon thee,
> And roll thee down from the rocks.
>
> (51.25)

As Jeremiah had earlier prophesied, "The iniquity of Israel shall be sought for, and *there shall be* none. . . . He shall thoroughly plead their cause, / That he may give rest to the land" (50.20–34). Babylon is now compared to Sodom and Gomorrah (50.40). In this sudden transformation, "Israel *hath* not *been* forsaken nor Judah / Of his God" (51.5), the literal phrasing, "For they are not widowed . . . from their God," *lō*ɔ*almān mē . . . ɔElōhāv*, restores the trope of marriage and all its implications to the prophesied reunification of God and his people.

Already by chapter 23, however, the restoration of the lineage of David is envisaged as a possibility. And the transpositions around birth pangs undergo further anguish. In these unnatural times, not only women but even men go through such pangs:

> Wherefore do I see every man
> With his hands on his loins, as a woman in travail,
> And all faces are turned into paleness?
>
> (30.6)

In the light of this theme, a new dimension is given to the legendary historical figure who is adduced, Rachel mourning for her lost children (31.15). Her refusal to be comforted recalls such fruitless anguish at a point where general consolation is in view. The image of the pains of a woman in travail is even applied to the old king of Babylon (50.43). And the prophet expresses his own anguish, through and from birth, in his recourse to such monstrous fusions:

> Cursed *be* the man who brought tidings
> To my father, saying,
> A man child is born unto thee;
> Making him very glad.
> And let that man be as the cities
> Which the Lord overthrew, and repented not:
> And let him hear the cry in the morning,
> And the shouting at noontide;
> Because he slew me not from the womb;
> Or that my mother might have been my grave,
> And her womb *to be* always great *with me.*
>
> (20.15–17)

The strange proposition of that last line, literally, "her womb be an everlasting conception," *raḥmāh harat ʿolam,* is climactic and inclusive, envisioning the nature of the body itself to serve as an image and an imagined drama for the deep frustration the prophet is voicing.

The narrative portions do not only prophesy with figuration, both explicit and implied; they also tell about prophecy. As a sort of counterbalance to the indirectness of the verses and an expansion of their register, they lay out the direct experience of the prophet, who suffers his message in the events of his life, periodically reporting a direct communication along the activated axis of converse between himself and God: "And the word of the Lord came unto me the second time, saying, What seest thou? And I said, I see a seething pot; and the face thereof *is* toward the north. Then the Lord said unto me, Out of the north an evil shall break forth upon all the inhabitants of the land" (1.13–14). This passage dimensionalizes what we understand as the structure of normal metaphor. A set of events is veiled in the future; it is the metaphor's tenor, but it expands the vehicle: the seething pot is made to stand actually, and without any necessary connection to these events, before the eyes of the prophet. There is no distinction between his real eye and his mind's eye here; and the pot lacks meaning until a connection emerges in the revealing words of God's discourse with the prophet whom he has elected to receive the vision. The prophet's role is also characterized by a series of metaphors: "For, behold, I have made thee this day a defended city, and an iron pillar, and brazen walls against the whole land. . . . And they shall fight against thee; but they shall not prevail against thee" (1.18–19). All this is suppler than the prose portions of Isaiah and, at the same time, of greater urgency. The suppleness is felt as an index of the greater urgency in the breaking of the pressure on Jeremiah into the rhythms of his utterance.

In keeping with the recurrences of motif through the book, the pot metaphor comes up again: Jeremiah has been ordered by the Lord to go to the house of the potter: "And the vessel that he made of clay was marred in the hand of the potter: so he made it again another vessel" (18.1). And then God speaks in interpretation: "O house of Israel, cannot I do with you as this potter? . . . Behold, as the clay *is* in the potter's hand, so *are* ye in mine hand" (18.6).

As in the case of the other, different use of the pot, this object lesson sets out a pattern that opens in many directions. To have Jeremiah observe the pot, which this time is clearly visible before the prophet, not only materializes God's relation to Israel but figures it as at once linear (one pot simply succeeds another) and cyclic (we come back to a pot after a pot). The figure simplifies and spatializes God's creation; and at the same time, the marred vessel sets up the possibility of an absolute and shocking discontinuity, one that remains puzzling. At another juncture, vessels undergo violence: "Every bottle shall be filled with wine. . . . I will fill all the inhabitants of this land . . . with drunkenness. And I will dash them one against another" (13.12–14). Here, in God's reported message, the bottles are a metaphor for persons—a metaphor that again breaks the even flow of time and the continuity of interrelationships between God and people on that vector of the triangle, using the prophet vector to communicate the new discontinuity and the absoluteness of the devastation: there is no redemptive future for a smashed bottle (though, in fact, the vision of the smashing turns out to be a phase).

Again, Jeremiah is enjoined to "break the bottle in the sight of the men that go with thee. . . . Even so will I break this people and this city" (19.10–11). The message is accompanied by a demonstration that is dire in its implications, while not yet catching up in its drama the very existence of the prophet. Later in the text, an earthen vessel serves simply as a container for the evidence of Jeremiah's symbolic purchase of land on the eve of disaster (32.6–15). Here the pot's figurative functions recede when it comes forward simply as an object of daily use. All these changes in the figural use of the pot evidence a dangerous instability underlying the powerful plasticity of the prophet's communication, an instability that makes his role more crucial along the active vector of the relation between prophet and people.[2]

All the more is this the case as the urgency and instability of the situation get exemplified in the vulnerability of the prophet, who includes in the text an account of how he suffers, directly and also figuratively, from an inability to get his message across. That inability becomes part of the message, as it indicates and exemplifies the frowardness of the people. Here Jeremiah's many interactions with distinct individuals in their vested roles differentiates him from Isaiah—first of all, with his scribe Baruch and, importantly, with the successive kings under whom he runs the gamut from trusted adviser to persecuted adversary. His relatives in Anathoth plot to kill him (chapters 12 and again 18). He is put in the stocks (chapter 20). He is first condemned to death in a verbal exchange that illustrates his opacity to the perverse people who see him as perverse: "This man *is* worthy to die; for he hath prophesied against this city, as ye have heard with your ears" (26.11). In its literal meaning, this remark begins even more bluntly: "Judgment of death for this man," *mišpat māvet la iš ha zeh*, a phrasing that counterbalances and countermands the fiercer and more complicated judgments of others. They, however, have already been adjudged, in a vivid expression, as confused in their very countenances, because they have not acted righteously along the axis of the connection of people to God: "Do they provoke me to anger? saith the Lord: *do they* not *provoke* themselves to the confusion of their own faces?" (7.19). Then Jeremiah is absolved (26.24). He performs the action, both symbolic and real, of defying the instability of property values under the invasion by buying the field in Anathoth (chapter 32). He is successively imprisoned (chapter

37), and then he is lowered down into a mire-filled cistern (chapter 38). As the Chaldeans prepare to carry out their final invasion, he tells the parable of the good figs (that go to Babylon) and the bad figs (that go to Egypt, 24); later, after his release and his recommendation to stay on under the puppet government of Gedalaiah, he is forced to go to Egypt himself (43). This is the least desirable of the three alternatives—Judah, Babylon, and Egypt—about which he has prophesied.

The role of Egypt does not stay symmetrical at the different points of time envisaged here. In the remote past, Egypt was the land of bondage out of which the Israelites went on the Exodus whose spirit they have now abandoned. In the present, it is a second-class power that a short-sighted policy will try to enlist against the Chaldeans, leading to Nebuchadnezzar's conquest of the Pharaoh's armies in 605 B.C.E. In the list of powers, the focus falls on Egypt (46.1–28) as the "Oracles of the Nations" unfold (chapters 46–51). All of the nations, eventually even Babylon, are prophesied to suffer similar devastation. In the proximate future, Egypt is a less-than-desirable refuge from exile in Babylon.

Jeremiah will die in Egypt. His fate at every point, down to the end, whether by direct example (prison, exile to Egypt) or by contrast (buying the field) reveals a certain symmetry with the repeated stages of the kingdom's fate vis-à-vis God. When Jeremiah buys a girdle as God directs him to do and stuffs it in a rock (13.1–7), he takes it out "marred" and "profitable for nothing." God moves that act itself, unaccompanied by any other utterance of the prophet, to the level of symbolic drama: "After this manner will I mar the pride of Judah, and the great pride of Jerusalem" (13.9). The act of buying while under guard the field connected to his inheritance encapsulates many of Jeremiah's relations and their significations (32.5–13). He uses "all the Jews that sat in the court of the prison" as loyal witnesses (32.12), then converts them to roles in the prophetic drama as this purchase spreads out into the prophecy of other redemptive land purchases (32.43). There is a symbolic and situational force in the action when King Jehoiakim cuts up Jeremiah's scroll and feeds it to the fire (36.20–26). This action only brings God's condemnation upon the king, and the scroll is replaced along with its words, which had "added besides unto them many like words" (36.32).

Prophet, people, and God are brought into anguished association; they are afflicted with a lack of communication that is expressed through the ambiguity of the word "burden," *maśśā*, which implies both a message and a weight to carry. Jeremiah instances both: the weight he carries is part of his message, and intricated into the message is the weight of God's communication about the burden:

> And when this people, or the prophet, or a priest, shall ask thee saying, What is the burden of the Lord, thou shalt then say unto them, What burden? I will even forsake you, saith the Lord. And *as for* the prophet, and the priest, and the people, that shall say The burden of the Lord, I will even punish that man and his house. . . . And the burden of the Lord shall ye mention no more, for every man's word shall be his burden, for ye have perverted the words of the living God, of the Lord of hosts our God. Thus shalt thou say to the prophet, What hath the Lord answered thee? and What hath the Lord spoken? But since ye say, The burden of the Lord, therefore thus saith the Lord; Because ye say this word, The burden of the Lord, and I have sent unto you saying, Ye shall not say, The burden of the Lord; Therefore, behold, I, even I, will utterly forget you. (23.33–39)

Here the repetitions play through the thrust of the word "burden," and the contradictions carry with them the severe injunction, itself a burden, that the very means has been shut off that would give recourse to activating the flow among prophet, people, and God. Any prophet will be punished as a false prophet—except for Jeremiah, who has been chosen as the channel for this utterance. His utterance does not so much tie the knot of a double bind as both announce and instance its inescapability.

The vision of time here, unlike that in the three stages of those who wrote under the signature of Isaiah, is disjunct and twofold. On the one hand, there is the steady decline through Jeremiah's forty years culminating in the destruction of Israel and the issuance into an oppressed Babylonian exile, a hard refuge in Egypt, or a humiliated continuance in the vassal state of Judah. On the other hand, the long process does not yield any of Isaiah's long-range perspective. Salvation for the people is only figured in Jeremiah's purchase of the devalued land. The salvation is envisioned at great intervals and mostly in glimpses (15.19–21; 22.4; 27.22; 29.10–14; 30.4–11; 31–33). For the people addressed by Isaiah, the memory of the Exodus is brought forward as an inspiration, whereas early in Jeremiah, the reminder of the Exodus serves only as a contrast:

> I remember thee, the kindness of thy youth,
> The love of thine espousals,
> When thou wentest after me in the wilderness
>
> (2.2)

And the reminder of the past goes on, not as an exhortation but as a grim contrast, through the next twelve verses, the more that the people are figured as a single person whose youth does not ripen into a wise old age. Their former devotion is in greater contrast for being characterized here by the intensive word "kindness," *ḥesed*. "Have I been a wilderness to Israel . . . ?" (2.31), God asks, fusing the wilderness wanderings of the Exodus with the "land of milk and honey" they have lost. There are reminders of Exodus, too, as well as perhaps of Elijah, in the description of God's visitation upon them, when the cloud will no longer be a guide before them but an omen against them:

> Behold, he shall come up as clouds,
> And his chariots *shall be* as a whirlwind:
> His horses are swifter than eagles.
>
> (4.13)

The reference to one of the earliest sanctuaries does not reassure: "my place which *was* in Shiloh" (7.12). Rather, this mention of Shiloh recalls an earlier disaster and the punishment for it by the destruction of that sanctuary. The "bones of the kings of Judah" and of all others in Jerusalem are to be dug up "out of their graves: And they shall spread them before the sun, and the moon, and all the host of heaven . . . for dung upon the face of the earth" (8.1–2). Here is a shocking time-arrest and subversion of normal time-pieties in burial, as well as a punishment by desecration.

The notion of "return," which comes up throughout Jeremiah, does not usually envisage a return from the future exile; rather, the people are caught in a dead end. "They refuse to return," and are involved in a "perpetual backsliding" (8.5). "Every one turned to his course, / As the horse rusheth into the battle" (8.6). Humankind's ignorant reversals of time are the more egregious by contrast with the understanding of animals, which "know" their "appointed times," including even the birds: the stork, the swallow, the crane, and the turtledove (8.7). "Thou art gone backward," God says to the people (15.6). "I will make this city as Tophet" (19.12) means that he will make it the opposite of a city, into a place of the dead victims of impious sacrifice (19.12–13; 7.31–34). When it is said that "If ye will not hear these words, I swear by myself, saith the Lord, that this house shall become a desolation" (22.5), God's swearing by his own name evidences a circularity and power that are to be cut off from the people. "For he shall return no more, / Nor see his native country" (22.10). The destruction plotted against Jeremiah parodies the Lord's destruction of the people:

> But I *was* like a lamb *or* an ox
> *That* is brought to the slaughter;
> And I knew not that they had devised devices against me, *saying*
> Let us destroy the tree with the fruit thereof,
> And let us cut him off from the land of the living,
> That his name may be no more remembered.
>
> (11.19)

But then, almost at once, a comparable fate is prophesied for the people, as often happens throughout Jeremiah:

> Behold, I will punish them:
> The young men shall die by the sword;
> Their sons and their daughters shall die by famine:
> And there shall be no remnant of them.
>
> (11.22–23)

Prophecy generally employs metaphors drawn on the normal activities and relations of a pastoral and agricultural society: husbandry, tending sheep, cultivating the vine, perpetuating the generations through marriage. These venerable, self-validating activities, often metaphorically associated with one another, are shown by Jeremiah to be disturbed and overturned: the fields become a wilderness, the vines fail, the people, figured as a woman, become prostitute. Jeremiah's recourse to such images does not reassure; it only intensifies the ghastliness of the picture: "I brought you into a plentiful country, / To eat the fruit thereof and the goodness thereof; . . . And [you] made mine heritage an abomination"

(2.7). "The pastors also transgressed against me" (2.8) uses "pastors," *rōˤîm*, to mean both shepherds and rulers, fusing the two and thereby incorporating the continuum between cultivation and governance into all the structure of the desert-fertility metaphor. In the idolatrous worship of the queen of heaven (44.18), that goddess seems to be responding effectively, but then this is on too simple a pattern, involving only women who are addressing her and not God. Soon the "virgin daughter of Egypt" finds no medicine or help (46.11).

Following Hosea and Isaiah, Jeremiah connects the "pollution" of the land to the defection of Israel, figured as a woman (3.1–21): "Thou hast polluted the land with thy whoredoms" (3.2). "She *is* wholly oppression in the midst of her" (6.6), comments Jeremiah, where "she" stands for the city. The figure spreads to include the prophet himself:

> O Lord, thou hast deceived me, and I was deceived:
> Thou art stronger than I, and hast prevailed:
> I am in derision daily,
> Every one mocketh me.

> (20.7)

Emphasizing that the verb used here, "deceived," *patah*, means "seduce a maid that is not betrothed," Harold Bloom reads Jeremiah as "betrothed to Yahweh in order to replace the harlot Jerusalem. . . . The daring of this similitude carries Jeremiah's defiance of the public opinion that nevertheless drives him toward breakdown."[3]

The fruit of the vine connects to the cycle of the seasons and to the theology of a bountiful God who provides this simple sustenance and delight to the people. Hence, its disruption is a prophetic theme, as it is in Isaiah 5, picked up and complicated by Jeremiah, who adduces grape gatherers in a residual comparison (49.49) and sees in his oracle about Moab an elaborate disruption of their famous vineyards, actually and symbolically, under the Babylonian invasion (48.10–13). The wines of their Sibnah region will fail (48.32–33). Later, Moab is "made drunk" (48.26), and there is punishment for drunkards (49.12). And the vineyard gets another metaphorical twist as it is stretched across the human generations, with a backward look this time at the perverse condition: "In those days they shall say no more, the fathers have eaten sour grapes / and the children's teeth are set on edge" (31.28). This cross-generational retribution, in the main thrust of Jeremiah's prophecy, has the force of hastening the dissolution of the triangle God-prophet-people and collapsing the time of the generational succession. Here, however, it is recalled to introduce the prophecy of a new covenant (31.31–40). "Is there no balm in Gilead?" the surprised prophet earlier asks (8.22), envisioning a general, utter failure of natural processes and associations.

Water is the omnipresent God-given aid to fertility: "When he uttereth his voice, *there is* a multitude of waters in the heavens, / And he causeth the vapors to ascend from the ends of the earth" (10.13). But here this majesty is evoked at a distance. Water is seen, prophetically and metaphorically, by Jeremiah as undergoing deflections from its role through the perverse actions of the Israelites:

> For my people have committed two evils;
> They have forsaken me the fountain of living waters,
> *And* hewed them out cisterns,
> Broken cisterns, that can hold no water.
>
> (2.13)

And later it is the water itself that is seen as bad:

> And now what hast thou to do in the way of Egypt,
> To drink the waters of Sihor?
> Or what hast thou to do in the way of Assyria
> To drink the waters of the river?
>
> (2.18)

For the prophet, water may serve not for fertilizing fields or for quenching thirst but for mourning:

> Oh that my head were waters,
> And mine eyes a fountain of tears,
> That I might weep day and night
> For the slain of the daughter of my people!
>
> (9.1)

Strangely contrastive are the images, presented through the voice of God, of the prophet as a tower set against the people as useless metals and as vehicles of metallurgy:

I have set thee *for* a tower *and* a fortress among my people,
That thou mayest know and try their way.
They *are* all grievous revolters,
Walking with slanders:
They are brass and iron;
They *are* all corrupters.
The bellows are burned,
The lead is consumed of the fire;
The founder melteth in vain:
For the wicked are not plucked away.
Reprobate silver shall *men* call them,
Because the Lord has rejected them.

(6.27–30)

Here intensity takes over and fuses normal craft, causing all to fail. "They are upright as a palm tree" (10.5), or more accurately, "like a pillar [a scarecrow] in a garden of cucumbers." This image once again takes the normal agricultural precautions out of a fertile setting in order to confound fertility. The normally useful scarecrow is transposed to a vain, lifeless idol carried in an idolatrous procession. And in a reversal, "The wind shall eat up all the pastors," *kōl rōᶜayīk tīrᶜeh rûaḥ* (22.22), the normal processes are condensed to echoes.

Having harped on the anguish of the ongoing present and touched on the blessedness of the future, Jeremiah can permute and syncopate these times. He puts blessing as a negative condition and in destructive terms (chapters 31 and 32). His text is that of one who sees the restoration of justice under seemingly impossible odds; it stresses the inadequacy of the people to meet the demands for the sort of uprightness and justice that would give them some chance to retain, or at least ultimately to restore, the old ways in which the natural cycles created by the Creator harmonized with his supernatural ones. The prophet has worked up to a point of transmitting an utterance of God that unbearably sets correspondence in the mode of dissymmetry: "Though they shall cry unto me, I will not hearken unto them" (11.11). The triangle of God, people, and prophet stands for a long time as unworkable, except in the prophet's transmission of a dialogue with God that sets up the theological dimensions of that unworkability in a manner later to be picked up in the confrontations of Job:

Righteous *art* thou, O Lord [*ṣadiq ʾatāh JHVH*],
When I plead with thee:
Yet let me talk with thee of *thy* judgments:
Wherefore doth the way of the wicked prosper?

(12.1)

As Joseph Blenkinsopp says about the visiting of the sins of parents on children and about God's possible injustice, the problem lies in

> the link between act and consequence. . . . With the destruction of Jerusalem in 586 B.C.E. . . . the problem . . . became insoluble. . . . It also found expression in a proverb . . . "the fathers have eaten sour grapes and the children's teeth are set on edge" (Jer 31:29–30; Ezek 18.2). . . . Given traditional religious beliefs, the massive disasters of the early sixth century B.C.E. could only mean that either Yahweh was powerless to prevent them happening or he had decided to punish his people in a manner totally out of proportion to their wrongdoing. Hence the accusation of injustice leveled against God—"the way of Yahweh is not just" (Ezek 18.25).

Blenkinsopp goes on to explain that "in the prophetic writings the link between sin and punishment—the latter in the form of political disaster—is the more prominent in that the prophets make extensive use of the political analogy of covenant with its associations of overlordship, binding obligations reinforced by curses, and the direct communication of the sovereign's will. . . . Sin brings about its effect on the sinner by virtue of its own inner dynamic. . . . The pattern can be seen in the condemnation of Saul by Samuel. . . . (1 Sam 15; cf. 13:7–15)."[4]

But all this political-religious intrication is a background of great power for Jeremiah, the ground along which the vectors of the God-people-prophet triangle operate. This prophet is not much concerned with working out theology or with opening new theological vistas, the method of the (later) Second and Third Isaiah. Rather, he condenses what he says, repeats it, brings it into the stresses of his own life and them into it. Jeremiah's "I will turn their mourning into joy" (31.13) echoes Isaiah's "oil of joy for mourning" (61.3) but does not fix it into so firm and apocalyptic a future.

4

"The Vision Is Touching the Whole Multitude"

Vision and History in Ezekiel

IN EZEKIEL'S PROPHECY, the sharp angle of history as it comes through the predominance of presented vision is couched in a particular mix of prose and poetry. While the prophet's life is close enough to that of Jeremiah to have overlapped it, and while there are echoes between the two prophets, there are large differences between the two in overall organization, in figural conception, and in dynamic posture, as well as in tonality and (to a lesser extent) in theological assumption.[1] Jeremiah's first call came in 626 B.C.E. during the long and fruitful reign of Josiah over the Southern Kingdom, a century after the fall of the Northern Kingdom to Sargon of Assyria in 722. He lived his whole life through the constant military pressures on Jerusalem, the defeat at the hands of the Babylonian Nebuchadnezzar in 597, and the destruction and general exile of the city in 586.

These circumstances were somewhat different for Ezekiel. Exiled in the first wave of 597, he received his first call in 592 "by the banks of Chebar" in Babylon. From the beginning, he wrote from "among the captives," *be tôk ha gôlāh*, literally, "in the midst of the exile" (1.1). The disaster had already happened, including what he mentions at once, the exile of the king (1.2). Writing down to 570, the prophet operates under an external condition devoid of the developmental tensions that the earlier prophets reflect. And as though by contrastive compensation, Ezekiel's prose casts itself in the form of a quasi-historical narrative, providing again and again precise dates for his utterances from the very opening of the book. In the statement "They and their fathers have transgressed against me even unto this very day," *ad 'eṣem ha yôm ha zeh* (2.3), the intensive word indicating the precision of the day is an idiomatic use of the word ʿeṣem, "bone," or "substance." The first phrase of the book adopts the standard formula of biblical narrative, the *vāv* consecutive, the conjunction "and" that keys a reversal of the ordinary tense of the verb that follows it. He takes regular recourse to this form: "Now it came to pass in the thirtieth year . . . " (1.1).

Moreover, while he does narrate some events, these narrations always center on the dramatic circumstances under which he utters a prophecy. So the state of affairs he addresses easily lends itself to the schematic matchings of analogy and antithesis that the poetic form of Hebrew parallelism is well equipped to embody. Yet he presents his statements prevailingly in prose; and when he does break into such verse, his sequences there do not enlist the full adaptiveness of Isaiah and Jeremiah. Moreover, strikingly at the beginning and protractedly toward the end, he concentrates in this prose on recounting elaborate and significant visions he has had.

The first vision concentrates and conflates symbolic elements, while the last one largely lays out, in specific detail and precise measurements, the vast Temple of the future, in a language that echoes the description of the actually built (and destroyed) Temple of Solomon (1 Kings 6.15–7.51). The sequentiality of historical narrative seems on the face of it to be at odds with the implied spatiality of such systematic presentation, and in that sense, the persistent echo of conventional biblical prose narrative serves to orient, and also to counter, the prophet's message. Yet the form does not so much go against the grain as set up the insistence of a ground in contrast to its figure.

From the beginning then, the visionary overview dominates the historical sequentiality that the narrative style seems to promise. This narrative style does lay out a sequence of events, not only in the regular narratives of the Pentateuch and the historical books but in such sequences as those by which Jeremiah recounts his developments under increasing pressure. In Ezekiel, the slackening of interaction between the people and God is dramatized by the initial absence (deferred to the second chapter) of any mention of retribution or of correspondences among the elements of this first symbolic vision. This elaborate vision comes forth at once to evidence and set the tonality for the majesty, mystery, and intricacy of God, as can be seen best when the passage is considered in its entirety:

1:4 And I looked, and, behold, a whirlwind came out of the north, a great cloud, and a fire infolding itself, and a brightness *was* about it, and out of the midst thereof as the color of amber, out of the midst of the fire. 5 Also out of the midst thereof *came* the likeness of four living creatures. And this *was* their appearance; they had the likeness of a man. 6 And every one had four faces, and every one had four wings. 7 And their feet *were* straight feet; and the sole of their feet *was* like the sole of a calf's foot; and they sparkled like the color of burnished brass. 8 And *they had* the hands of a man under their wings on their four sides; and they four had their faces and their wings. 9 Their wings *were* joined one to another; they turned not when they went; they went every one straight forward. 10 As for the likeness of their faces, they four had the face of a man, and the face of a lion, on the right side: and they four had the face of an ox on the left side; they four also had the face of an eagle. 11 Thus *were* their faces: and their wings *were* stretched upward; two *wings* of every one *were* joined one to another, and two covered their bodies. 12 And they went every one straight forward: whither the spirit was to go, they went; *and* they turned not when they went. 13 As for the likeness of the living creatures, their appearance *was* like burning coals of fire, *and* like the appearance of lamps: it went up and down among the living creatures; and the fire was bright, and out of the fire went forth lightning. 14 And the living creatures ran and returned as the appearance of a flash of lightning.

15 Now as I beheld the living creatures, behold one wheel upon the earth by the living creatures, with his four faces. 16 The appearance of the wheels and their work *was* like unto the color of a beryl: and they four had one likeness: and their appearance and their work *was* as it were a wheel in the middle of a wheel. 17 When they went, they went upon their four sides: *and* they turned not when they went. 18 As for their rings, they were so high that they were dreadful; and their rings *were* full of eyes round about them four. 19 And when the living creatures went, the wheels went by them: and when the living creatures were lifted up from the earth, the wheels were lifted up. 20 Whithersoever the spirit was to go, they went, thither *was their* spirit to go; and the wheels were lifted up over against them: for the spirit of the living creature *was* in the wheels. 21 When those went, *these* went; and when those stood, *these* stood; and when those were lifted up from the

earth, the wheels were lifted up over against them: for the spirit of the living creature *was* in the wheels. 22 And the likeness of the firmament upon the heads of the living creature *was* as the color of the terrible crystal, stretched forth over their heads above. 23 And under the firmament *were* their wings straight, the one toward the other: every one had two, which covered on this side, and every one had two, which covered on that side, their bodies. 24 And when they went, I heard the noise of their wings, like the noise of great waters, as the voice of the Almighty, the voice of speech, as the noise of a host: when they stood, they let down their wings. 25 And there was a voice from the firmament that *was* over their heads, when they stood, *and* had let down their wings.

26 And above the firmament that *was* over their heads *was* the likeness of a throne, as the appearance of a sapphire stone: and upon the likeness of the throne *was* the likeness as the appearance of a man above upon it. 27 And I saw as the color of amber, as the appearance of fire round about within it, from the appearance of his loins even upward, and from the appearance of his loins even downward, I saw as it were the appearance of fire, and it had brightness round about. 28 As the appearance of the bow that is in the cloud in the day of rain, so *was* the appearance of the brightness round about. This *was* the appearance of the likeness of the glory of the Lord. And when I saw it, I fell upon my face, and I heard a voice of one that spake.

2:1 And he said unto me, Son of man, stand upon thy feet, and I will speak unto thee. 2 And the spirit entered into me when he spake unto me, and set me upon my feet, that I heard him that spake unto me.

Ezekiel's initial vision concatenates into an unusual relational *syntax* a number of symbolic elements of strongly marked *diction*, all of them both connected to and displaced from what immediately follows, the flat monitory declaration of 2.3, "I send thee to the children of Israel, a rebellious nation." All these constituent symbols of the vision exhibit the intensity of their figuration through the frequency and loaded significance of their appearance in other biblical contexts. These symbols have, as well, a wide distribution in the Near East and, indeed, among humanity at large. Frequently pointed out are the winged beasts in Babylonian iconography, the celestial eyes among the Egyptians, and so on. So each of these symbols taken separately is an element of diction. Yet Ezekiel's symbols, in the syntax of their concatenations, do not lend themselves to any rich parallel with the symbol systems of neighboring cultures.[2]

These elements of the first vision, in the sequence given here, are: a whirlwind ("from the north"—itself a historically and symbolically loaded area), a cloud, a fire, a brightness the color of amber (or electrum), four living creatures with faces, wings and feet ("like the sole of a calf's foot"), and the color of brass (or polished bronze). These creatures have, compositely, each a head squared with the faces of a man, a lion, an ox, and an eagle—creatures that figure elsewhere in Ezekiel: the man by frequent reference, the ox by the implication of agricultural activity frequently mentioned, and the eagle and the lion by the later runs of disjunct symbolization devoted to them (chapters 17 and 19).[3] Then there are burning coals, lamps, and a fire giving way to lightning—all of these melding into wheels (1.15), their rims ("rings") set with eyes (1.18) under a "firmament" (or "fixed platform") of crystal (1.22).[4] Then comes a noise "of waters" conflating the voice of the Almighty, of speech, and of a host; and then a throne, on which is a man, and a rainbow, equaling the "glory of the Lord" (1.24–26).

There is a persistent horizontality to this vision: "they went every one straight forward" (1.12). And then there is a verticality, since the whole complex series, all the way up to the firmament, stands beneath that firmament, while the throne stands above it. The whole unfolds and mutates: the fire gives way to lightning, the creatures to wheels. Already stated in 1.4 were wind and cloud and a fire that "infolds itself," *mitlaqaḥat*. Out of the midst came, "like the color [*ᶜēn*, "eye"] of amber," "the likeness of four living creatures." Four faces on each "infolds" and repeats the succession. By 1.16, all condenses to a wheel within a wheel; a wheel, *ʾôphan*, becomes the "appearance of the wheels."

The sense of dynamic force in these charged likenesses builds through the deep shifts of figuration, as there is a recursion of "man" and of "amber" (1.26–27), and these deep shifts press the sense of what

the figuration comes to, which is also qualified in the prophet's modification of his depiction by the term "likeness," a modification also
adopted later in the Book of Daniel.

The anthropological mix of traditional elements in this vision does
not attain to the systematic presentation of an end of time opening on
timelessness, as in Revelations, though it moves in that direction. And
here, too, the whirlwind and the fire, the faces and the winged creatures, the wheels and the eyes, the spirit and the firmament and the
throne stand free, for the time being, of other sequences in history, of
direct allegorical application. The prophet simply "saw" them in "visions." The description is rendered by a word that simply repeats the
verb "to see," *rāāh*. This is very close to the word that comes up several
times almost at once, "appearance," *mar²eh*. While *rāāh* is used for a religious vision in the Pentateuch, the more regular emphatic or hieratic
word for vision that one would have expected, *ḥāzāh*, does not occur until much later, with an application that could spread beyond its much
simpler immediate context through the whole book: "This vision is
touching the multitude" (7.13). That same, more emphatic word then
enters Ezekiel's discourse frequently and notably, as if to test it, in connection with the false visions of false prophets in chapter 13.

The prophet also speaks of "the word of the Lord" (1.3) that has
come to him; but that term, *dāvār*, also means "thing" or "fact," and so
it does not have to imply verbal mediation: it can indicate just the fact
of the transparent vision Ezekiel is here presenting.[5] The language in
which he presents it, indeed, faces two ways. It faces towards transpar-
ency in its low-keyed, highly charged terminology. But it also faces towards its own incapacity and the necessity of mediation. Again
and again, this vision narrative has recourse to no fewer than four
terms of approximation, each of them repeated many times: (1) "like,"
(2) "appearance," (*mar²eh*), (3) "eye," "look," or "surface," (*²ēn*, rendered
as "color" in the King James Version above), and (4) "likeness" (*demût*).
The language of the narrative keeps touching on and combining these
terms of qualification.

Such qualifications persist in the later vision of chapters 8–11 that
repeats some of these symbolic elements. In a discourse that for its poetic passages bases itself fundamentally on the parallelism of repetition, these narrative repetitions, indeed, take on the rhetorical emphasis

of a much varied, long-range parallelism. The man of amber and fire, and later the cherubim, reappear; and, like the first time, such terms as "appearance of a likeness" and similar phrases modulate the vision theologically. The "form or appearance of a hand" (8.3) takes the prophet by a lock of hair and puts him between earth and heaven. But this time he is brought to Jerusalem, and the whole vision intertwines with reactions to the sins of Israel, as also happens in the intervening chapters. Abominations of actual idolatry are being addressed, including worship of the Babylonian vegetation god Tammuz and worship of the sun. When the cherubim vision is repeated, as Ezekiel recognizes (10.15, 20), men or angels clothed in linen are to slaughter the sinners. The linen-clothed man holding a stylus is enjoined to take fire from the wheels of the cherubim. Mixed in here is an allegorical description more akin to those in the intervening chapters. "Your slain . . . *are* the flesh and this *city is* the caldron," they say (11.7), and God says not (11.11), thus invoking the prophetic dialectic of successive retribution and redemption.

The disjunction of the first vision from the admonishment to the Israelites simultaneously underscores the admonishment by a magnificent display of countervailing power and qualifies it by an underlying suggestion, to be stated much later, that in the long range and broad sweep of such power, any reconciliation might be possible. Within itself, the procession of whirlwind and cloud, winged creatures and wheels, throne and firmament mounts a freestanding array of symbols whose significances seem to draw power from the unapplied openness of their significations.

A very different significative structure obtains in the series of symbolizations that follow between the first vision and the second appearance of the cherubim.

As Walter Zimmerli says, "The elements of vision and of drastic symbolic actions . . . appear very much more strongly in Ezekiel than in the other great writing prophets. Clapping the hands (6:11; 21:19), stamping the feet (6:11), the performance of actions the outward accomplishment of which is often hardly conceivable, and above all the dramatic endurance of translation to Jerusalem and other places and long range vision, as well as bodily paralysis and inability to speak, give to this prophet a strangeness of psychic experience."[6]

Such symbolic actions begin with Ezekiel's actual eating of the scroll that records his vision (2.9–3.3), something he is to do before addressing the Israelites directly. The scroll, unusual because it is written on both sides to emphasize the abundance of the divine message, is full of "lamentations and mourning and woe" (2.10).[7] Still, when the prophet eats it, the taste is "sweet as honey"—a contradiction that encapsulates a suspension of the painful interaction between prophet and people in favor of a direct exaltation in the contact between prophet and the commanding God. Here are no coals of fire on the tongue as there were with Isaiah and no fire in the mouth as with Jeremiah, but an absorptive, gustatory pleasure.

The prophet now intimately foregrounds his own body. This time he does not see, and in fact, the scroll disappears. Rather, he acts, and the disjunction between the sky vision from God to prophet and the admonishment from God to the Israelites has reappeared in the form of an opposition between their sorrow and the prophet's joy. There is also an opposition of timing. The joy of the taste of the scroll is immediately present, a single condensed experience, while what is written on the scroll, as present as it would be in a Book of Life, treats the future—presumably of the Israelites—as though it were a past, in an unspecified, long range of "lamentations and mourning and woe." This long-range sorrow stands itself in significative opposition to the dating, precise to the day, offered for sequenced events throughout the book.

Prophetic enactments in real life with allegorical extrapolations to social events are carried out by Jeremiah when he shatters the jar, wears the yoke, and breaks it, and when he buys devalued land; and by Hosea, when he takes a prostitute as a wife and names his children after the woes of Israel. Ezekiel runs through a series of enactments, changing the figuration at each turn. And he goes further than the simple sign-actions of the earlier prophets that Zimmerli describes: "Already in pre-classical prophecy we can see how Ahijah of Shiloh hands the kingship over ten of the tribes of Israel to Jeroboam in the ten parts of his torn cloak (1 Kings 11:29–31). Zedekiah assures Ahab of victory over Syria by the iron horns on his head (1 Kings 22:11). Elisha enables Joash to gain victory over Syria by means of 'the arrows of Yahweh's victory' which Joash shoots through the open window towards the east (2 Kings 13:14–19)."[8]

Ezekiel's sign-actions are more complicated than are these earlier enactments—more complicated in figuration and more far-reaching in consequence, as well as more dynamic in execution. Instead of speaking, he is commanded to draw on a tile a representation of the besieged Jerusalem (4.1–3) and to set an iron pan "for a wall between thee and the city." This action mimes carrying out a future action. Taking the tile and building the model lies midway between the dumbness just inflicted on Ezekiel and the prophetic speaking or "pouring forth" (a root meaning of *nāvî*, "prophet") expected of him by role and by later specific command. His prophesy is more passive than that of his predecessors. And his puzzling dumbness, cast through much of the text, has been interpreted as God's constraint upon him to give an utterance only when God specifically commands him to do so.[9]

On the tile, he silently creates a miniature "real" vision rather than receiving a celestial one. This act of drawing is coupled with another physical action, a more arduous one, referring to the present and timed to the day. The prophet is to lie on his side to indicate the time of suffering: "This shall be a sign to the house of Israel. . . . *According* to the number of the days that thou shalt lie upon it thou shalt bear their iniquity" (4.3–5), a day for a year, 390 days for the 390 years of the vanished Northern Kingdom. Then in 4.6, turned upon his other side, he symbolizes the same equivalence for Judah, forty days for forty years. Using his own body, he will "lay the iniquity of Israel upon it" (4.4). The whole dynamic here stands out saliently in its contrastive, metaphoric, gapped structure with the other presentations and metaphoric structures.

Next, he is given a bread recipe to prepare, its ingredients again measured to a number of days, but its significance is obscured until the final commandment (4.12), that the bread be baked with human dung. He is to do this "in their sight," and the significance is spelled out in the injunction "Even thus shall the children of Israel eat their defiled bread among the Gentiles, whither I will drive them" (4.13). After Ezekiel protests this violation of taboo, God modifies the fuel to the usual cow dung. There ensues a dialogue not between Ezekiel and the Israelites but between Ezekiel and God. The meal, in any case, will symbolize how the Israelites will be forced to eke out their food and "consume away for their iniquity" (4.17).

In chapter 5, the symbolism shifts again and so does the figurative structure. Shaving off his hair and weighing it, Ezekiel is to burn one third "in the midst of the city" and later is to burn more; he is to take another third and "smite about it with a knife" and is to scatter the last third to the wind (5.2). Now the hair stands directly for the Israelites, as is shown by God's statement that, in each case, these actions are matched to his actions upon them, while dire events are spelled out through the rest of the chapter.

In their seeming arbitrariness and their contextual totalizations, these shifting enactments have the character of what is called in our time "street theater," as B. Lang has characterized the dramatizations in Ezekiel.[10] After this shifting sequence of symbolizations, Ezekiel is enjoined to prophesy directly—and now God will carry out dire actions that are at once symbolic and actual. He will lay the dead carcasses before their idols (6.5) and scatter bones and altars.

In the regular poetic run of chapter 17, the prophet responds to the allegorically veiled message of God, "Son of man, put forth a riddle, and speak a parable unto the house of Israel" (17.2). This parable of the two eagles and the "vine" from the top of the cedar stands for a series of political actions: Nebuchadnezzar, the "great eagle" is tricked by the Israelite Zedekiah into intrigues with the second great eagle, the reigning Pharaoh; and the "vine" (cedar shoot) of Israel is transplanted, first destructively, and then fruitfully, while Nebuchadnezzar conquers Pharaoh. Now these symbols come from two domains; the eagle regularly stands for majesty and power; the vine, already presented in chapter 15 but common throughout the prophets, symbolizes the fruitfulness of the regular agricultural cycle as it may be applied to a healthy and prosperous national succession.[11] The eagles and the vine somewhat spatialize this action, as though its time frame were already set. The verse is simple.

In its actual presentation, the introductory statement intensifies with cognate accusatives. It says, literally, "riddle a riddle and parable a parable," a phrasing that has the effect of conflating the two terms. The coupling of these terms makes them general and nonpropositional, even though the verbal emphasis on both is strong. "Riddle a riddle," in addition to its rhetorical emphasis, may be taken to underscore the puzzle of the *prima facie* lack of association between vine and eagle and the impenetrability of their connection before it is solved in 17.14–23. Once it has been solved, the riddle becomes a parable but with a fusion that appears in the conclusion of 17.24: "All the trees of the field shall know that I the Lord have brought down the high tree." This combines the tenor and the vehicle of the parable, a cedar tree, in another riddling utterance. Like most of Ezekiel's verse runs, this one is simple and recursive, more unmodulated in progression than the verse of other prophets, even the early Amos.

The vine is picked up again, and in verse, after a long intervening prose chapter (18) quoting a retributive and moralizing God on the sins of Israel. Chapter 19 returns to verse, a verse the voice of God describes, in the 3:2 measure of *quinah*, as "lamentation." Such a measure is a powerful inducement toward the reduction of the statement to a single tone. And the verse of chapter 17, and generally of Ezekiel, is already simple in its evolutions. It is as though the prophet's major expressive energy has gone into figuration rather than into poetic modulations, a symbolization in the verse that could reverberate from the tremendous initial prose vision of chapter 1 and lead up to the concluding, expansive one of chapters 40–48. In chapter 17, the eagle and the vine are brought into surprising conjunction. Now, in chapter 19, at a kind of climax, it is a lion and a vine: "Thy mother *is* like a vine in thy blood / planted by the waters" (19.10). The mother is a lion, probably Judah, though the powerful wrenching of the initial allegory produces confusion among commentators. Once set, this vine metaphor continues for the remaining four, fairly long verses of the chapter. It seems to lose the connection to blood, but it picks up one to a "rod" that moves from plant to sceptre: "She had strong rods" (19.11), "But she was plucked up . . . and the east wind dried up her fruit" (19.12), "Now she *is* planted in the wilderness" (19.13), "She hath no strong rod *to be* a sceptre" (19.14).

In the flow of this prophecy, the prose sections predominate too strongly to function as introductions, or even as alternations, as does the prose interspersed through Isaiah and more prominently through Jeremiah. Here the key shifts distinctly from monitory prose narrative to verse lamentation—and back again to prose in chapter 20 ("And it came to pass in the seventh year . . . " [20.1]). These shifts have the effect of blocks of mutual qualification. Warning cuts off, complements, and counters lament, as eagle does vine before and lion does vine afterward. These large-scale "prior" qualifications by verbal form and by figural mutation coexist with, and possibly even coordinate with, a tendency in this prophet for the verse units to stay fairly simple—without the tensile modifications in Isaiah or even Jeremiah.

There is a startling energy packed into the symbols of "Thy mother *is* like a vine in thy blood"—with its proto-Freudian view of the powerful lion mother and her effect on her offspring, its protosurrealist distortions, its intense merging of agricultural cycle (vine), dynasty (the lion as queen), family (the lion as mother), and its hint in "blood" of the retributions just mentioned in chapter 18. The echo of blood, indeed, continues through the whole book, written in the face of constant arbitrary violence and under the shadow of prior military defeats. Here it is all compressed into the figures of this single verse. The conclusion of the chapter dwells on the vine figure, as discussed above, by narrative extension rather than by strong mutations of the parallelism. And most of this chapter, from the beginning, characteristically dwells even longer on the image of the three lions, without at any point modifying the obliquity of the allegory to identify the mother lion as Judah and the cubs as the deported kings Jehoiachin and Jehoahaz:

> Moreover, take thou up a lamentation for the princes of Israel, 2
> And say,
>
> What *is* thy mother? A lioness:
> She lay down among lions,
> She nourished her whelps
> Among young lions.
> 3   And she brought up one of her whelps:
> It became a young lion,
> And it learned to catch the prey;
> It devoured men.
> 4   The nations also heard of him;
> He was taken in their pit,
> And they brought him with chains
> Unto the land of Egypt.

5   Now when she saw that she had waited,
And her hope was lost,
Then she took another of her whelps,
And made him a young lion.
6   And he went up and down among the lions,
He became a young lion,
And learned to catch the prey,
And devoured men.
7   And he knew their desolate palaces,
And he laid waste their cities;
And the land was desolate, and the fulness thereof,
By the noise of his roaring.

(19.1–7)

Here, too, the keynote of a symbol-veiled narration simply gives the progressions. The parallelism is in the form either of simple identifying synonymy, such as in 2a, 2b, 3a, 5b, 6a, and 6b; or of narrative amplification, as is found in all the other verses quoted. The narrative substructure keeps the repetitions from gaining the stepped-up cumulations of staircase parallelism, further carried out by the near identity between all of verses 3 and 6. The only difference between these two verses, the only variation, lies in "he went up and down [among the lions]" of verse 6, where the single word *yithalēk*, here translated by five English words, is the reflexive and inflected form of *halak*, "to walk," a form that implies "walk with majesty, proudly and self-absorbedly."[12]

Again, after the long prose retribution narrative of chapter 20, the verse changes its metaphor, this time to a sword (21.8–30). The whole run can be conceived as being in a delayed parallelism to the lion chapter, since it applies to the same, or at least to similar, events:

And thou, son of man, prophesy and say, Thus saith the Lord God concerning the Ammonites, and concerning their reproach; even say thou,

The sword, the sword *is* drawn:
For the slaughter *it is* furbished,
To consume because of the glittering:
While they see vanity unto thee,

While they divine a lie unto thee,
To bring thee upon the necks of *them that are* slain,
Of the wicked, whose day is come,
When their iniquity *shall have* an end.
Shall I cause *it* to return into his sheath?
I will judge thee in the place where thou wast created,
In the land of thy nativity.
And I will pour out mine indignation upon thee;
I will blow against thee in the fire of my wrath,
And deliver thee into the hand of brutish men,
And skilful to destroy.
Thou shalt be for fuel to the fire;
Thy blood shall be in the midst of the land.

(21.28–2)

The play from "glittering" to "vanity" and the shift from sword to fire space through repetitions and equivalences that underscore and even absolutize each metaphor as it comes along—eagle and vine, lion and vine and rod, sword and fire—even though a closer look at the function and significative substructure of each symbol would reveal shifts of application. This is true, too, for the large visions, recounted unfailingly in prose.

At the pitch of his run through the fates of nations (chapters 25–32), a prophetic set piece whose like is to be found in several other prophets, Ezekiel does ring changes on his parallel units:

25 The ships of Tarshish did sing of thee in thy market:

And thou wast replenished, and made very glorious
In the midst [lit. "heart"] of the seas.
26 Thy rowers have brought thee
Into great waters:
The east wind hath broken thee
In the midst [lit. "heart"] of the seas.
27 Thy riches, and thy fairs, thy merchandise,
Thy mariners, and thy pilots,
Thy calkers, and the occupiers of thy merchandise,
And all thy men of war, that *are* in thee,

And in all thy company which *is* in the midst of thee,
Shall fall into the midst of the seas
In the day of thy ruin.
28 The suburbs shall shake
At the sound of the cry of thy pilots.
29 And all that handle the oar,
The mariners, *and* all the pilots of the sea,
Shall come down from their ships,
They shall stand upon the land;
30 And shall cause their voice to be heard against thee,
And shall cry bitterly,
And shall cast up dust upon their heads,
They shall wallow themselves in the ashes:
31 And they shall make themselves utterly bald for thee,
And gird them with sackcloth,
And they shall weep for thee with bitterness of heart
And bitter wailing.
32 And in their wailing they shall take up a lamentation for thee,
And lament over thee, *saying*,
What *city is* like Tyrus, like the destroyed
In the midst of the sea?
33 When thy wares went forth out of the seas,
Thou filledst many people;
Thou didst enrich the kings of the earth
With the multitude of thy riches and of thy merchandise.
34 In the time *when* thou shalt be broken by the seas
In the depths of the waters,
Thy merchandise and all thy company
In the midst of thee shall fall.

(27.25–34)

Sustaining these verses is a hierarchy of coherences—and also, in a sense, of large-scale parallelisms: of activity, nation by nation; of prosperity, nation compared with Israel; of cosmic testimony to Creation, the seas like the skies of the first vision.[13] Entering as well are the small-scale coherences, such as those that come through the repetitions on "beauty" earlier in the chapter, praised in verse 3, picked up in verse

4—"Thy builders have perfected thy beauty"—and picked up again at verse 11. Breaking into verse from prose at the point quoted, the whole reverberates in the mode of a song about Tyre sung by the ships of Tarshish, a city at the other end of the Mediterranean. Tyre is at the "heart" of the seas, according to the literal expression, *lev*. This emphasizes not only the spatial centrality of Tyre's activity, but also its intimacy-in-prosperity with Creation. Corresponding to this song of Tarshish, though, is the "cry of thy pilots," at which "the suburbs shall shake"—and the voice will be heard against Tyre, changing the song to what is finally named as a "lamentation" in verse 32.

By the time of the lamentation, the expression "in the heart of the seas" is no longer used. It has now become, literally, "in the midst," *be tôk*, of what has now shrunk to the simple "sea." "The seas" are in the past of verse 33 and the declaration carries through "the time *when* thou shalt be broken by the seas / In the depths of the waters" (27.34). The success has led to drowning, and marine prosperity has given way to shipwreck on the high seas. Tyre is no longer sustained "at the heart of the seas." Now the midst signifies ruin: "all thy company / In the midst of thee shall fail"; the midst turns back on the failing city. Space, however, still undulates into view: "The *suburbs* shall shake / At the sound of the cry of thy pilots" (27.28).

In 27.34, "*depths* of the waters" is an ominous phrase with nearly the same designation as "the heart of the seas" but with an opposite tone. The effect carries through the Mediterranean world: in 27.35, "The inhabitants of the isles [i.e., a distant location] shall be astonished at thee." In the next chapter, more directly, there is an injunction to lament the king of Tyre (28.2), and as the book goes on, Tyre is twinned with Sidon (28.20); then the restoration of the scattered Israel comes quickly into view (28.24–26).

Such expansions contract in the most cumulative, simplest, and theologically starkest of the prose visions, the Valley of Dry Bones in chapter 37. For this vision, too, schematizes desolation and restoration into a simple before-and-after form. Ezekiel, "Son of man," is "set down in a valley which *was* full of bones" (37.1). God asks him to prophesy to them, and as Ezekiel speaks to them, God first shakes them, unites them, and cloaks them with "sinews, flesh and skin" (37.6). Then, at the second act of prophesy commanded from Ezekiel, God breathes life into the bones and they stand, "an exceeding great army" (37.10). In chapter 36, there was a constant repetition of restorations, fortified by their parallelism to each other and, emphatically, to restoration promises. To these promises, the Valley of Dry Bones stands in a sort of antithetical parallelism—as well as in synonymous parallelism to the mentions of the desolation that is to be overcome and to the overcoming that comes about when the bones take on life. This vision pulls together the earlier references to bones, such as "their iniquities shall be on their bones" (32.27). In chapter 37, the bones are mentioned suddenly. Their presence ups the ante of restoration, since desolation cannot have gone further. The Valley of Bones, at this point, recapitulates the whole fate of Israel and the arbitrariness of the impending mercy.

Ezekiel is presented as something like an instrumental agent. He is to *prophesy* to the *bones*, and then the wind or spirit comes to vivify them in a magic revival. It is not possible to ascertain the exact status of this vision. While far simpler than the one in the first chapter, it is in some ways more obscure. Is it a metaphor, and if so, in what sense? If it simply means that the Israelites were destroyed and restored, what is the effect of the charnel valley? Is it an exaggeration, a proleptic eschatology, a mere shock presentation, or something of all these? In 37.6, there is an echo of Creation (as Zimmerli says ad loc): "And I will lay sinews upon you, and will bring up flesh upon you, and cover you with skin, and put breath in you, and ye shall live." In 37.16–20, God commands that Ezekiel take sticks together into fasces to stand for the union of the tribes of Israel. This bit of drama seems to mime the prior rejoining of the bones, but why is it necessary? Yet, for all these ambiguities, there is a clarity of signification in the very obscurity of this presentation.

"Visionary experiences," remarks Zimmerli, "are also to be found in earlier written prophecy (Amos 7:1–8; 8:1–2; 9:1–4; Isaiah 6; Jeremiah 4:23–26; 24:1–10). The distinctive feature of Ezekiel's visions lies in the fact that the prophet himself is, in large measure, active and shares strongly in the event."[14] Moreover, Ezekiel does so with an alternation of passive vision and active prophecy, presence and absence, muteness and speech, that matches the cycled reversals and repetitions-with-variation of the prophecy itself. In 1.3, the reference to him already changes from the first to the third person, and already he has shifted his focus more than do Isaiah or Jeremiah.[15] His first vision comes after a whirlwind, as does Elijah's, but that prophet's "still small voice" does not enter into anything comparable to the universe of Ezekiel's vision or its complicated sequel. As for the roles Ezekiel assumes, surprisingly it is only at this date that he first identifies himself as a *cohen*, a priest (1.3). Then he is addressed as "Son of man" (2.3), a recursive and exemplary identification that, as G. A. Cooke points out, "has a special emphasis in Ezekiel." "As a creature he receives from his Creator a designation which is all that a mere man can claim; as a prophet he is the mouthpiece and nothing more, of the divine will."[16] Shortly thereafter, Ezekiel names himself as a prophet whom the people will have to recognize (2.5). In 3.17, a third role (a fourth role, if "Son of man" is counted separately) comes into view, that of "watchman," *ṣopheh*. And all of these roles are in contrast to the occasional dumbness of the prophet, such as he experienced before the fall of Jerusalem (24.27). Given the cosmic sphere of the prophet's relations and the urgent dynamism of his connections, such terms as "watchman" are pregnant with extensibility. Grounded in a homely village role, the watchman also carries the possibility of a quasi-metaphysical survey of the deep justice he is perpetually, and perforce, critically evoking. In Emmanuel Levinas's terms, the prophet's very existence equivocates deeply, to begin with, between the categories "same" and "other."[17] As representative of the people, their spokesman, the prophet rests on his sameness. But as one who is awake while they are sleeping, who can voice what they are evading, he is other. Amos, the new prophet come north from the Southern Kingdom, already permutes the equivocation between same and other.

At 20.49, Ezekiel ends a long chapter consisting of a message received from God by stating his weariness with parables: "Ah Lord God! they say of me, Doth he not speak parables."[18] Here he seems to emphasize the parable element in his utterances. At one moment (3.24–4.8), he is both bound and silenced, yet he is not oppressed and scorned like Jeremiah. After this series of utterances, God will make him dumb (3.24–26).[19] He falls into deep silence at the death of his wife; yet at other times, the Israelites come in delegations to his dwelling to receive his prophecy. Earlier (3.18), God has said he will "require" the blood of the wicked out of Ezekiel's hand, "if thou givest him not warning [*zāhar*, "call to remembrance"]."

Still earlier (3.13–15), the prophet reported that "the spirit *lifted me up* at the *noise* of the wings," and then he was made silent for seven days on his return to the exiles by the Chebar, evoking an obscurity of allegorizing rather than a straightforward matching in this whole elaborate procedure of bodily mimesis. At 33.22, the end of Ezekiel's dumbness is connected with the message that Jerusalem is smitten. Still, he is told early that "the house of Israel will not love to hear thee for they will not love to hear me" (3.7). (The expression *lo yºovu li šemˤa*, which could be rendered "do not like to hear," is translated simply "will not hearken" in the King James Version.) "Behold," God goes on to say, "I have made thy face strong against their faces" (3.8), and for the moment, it would seem that the triangle of prophet, God, and people has been locked along all the axes of its vectors, all the more so because God immediately specifies that "as an adamant harder than flint have I made thy forehead" (3.9). At 3.11, the question is still open whether they will "hear and forebear," *yeḥdālû*. In chapter 6, God tells him to prophesy to nature, "to the mountains and to the hills, to the rivers and the valleys." But this command reverberates to the people, because at once he adds, "Behold I, *even* I will bring a sword upon you, and I will destroy your high places" (6.3).

As far into the book as 7.26, Ezekiel's access to the Israelites is distanced by subprophetic activities: "mischief shall come upon mischief and rumor shall be upon rumor; then shall they seek a vision of the prophet; but the law shall perish from the priest, and counsel from the ancients." And later (22.28), false prophets will get into the mix, prophets who are "envisioning vanity," *ḥōzîm šºav*.

Again envisioning the man of amber, in chapter 8 the prophet relates that "the spirit lifted me up between earth and heaven" (8.3) and he is temporarily moved to Jerusalem. At 24.19–28, the death of Ezekiel's wife is placed (literally) in the sequence, tied in dramatically with his speaking, as was the wife of Hosea. Then, when he begins speaking again, his attention is sequenced outward and he undertakes his prophecies against the Ammonites, Tyre, and many others. At 37.9, it takes prophecy to summon the breath in the bones. "Prophesy," as a refrain-command, keeps setting up the dialectic of interactive relations among prophet, God, and people. Like Isaiah, he has a "burden" (12.9).

Finally, he announces, "The vision is touching the whole multitude." The dynamic vectors of this dialectic will be perceived as having taken over—and the more totally because they have functioned unstably with various distancings throughout the book. The last, long chapters on the restoration of the Temple speak of no further modification and are therefore not open-ended like Isaiah and Jeremiah.

Along each of the axes of the interactive triangle prophet-God-people, the power of the utterance is invoked most absolutely when it is designated as one that has issued verbatim from God, a "saying of the Lord," *neˀûm Adonai*—as quite often happens in Ezekiel, as well as in other prophets (twenty-seven times in Amos). The prophet's power, both charismatic and institutional, derives from an attunement to the developing will of the Lord and from a capacity to transmit directives and visions. He speaks under the danger of being threatened by the competitive utterances of false prophets. And the performative carry-through is always hovering at the brink of incompletion. The people tend to be resistant to changing their ways. The power of the people derives from whatever fundament of virtue they can draw on to enter into such power relations in the political world as they can astutely and righteously manage.

Typically, the surviving Southern Kingdom of Judah has failed at managing this kind of power because its loss of righteousness means it can offer no counterbalance to the vastly superior military might of the Babylonians or even the Egyptians. But those other powerful peoples, of course, do not operate in a zone free of the power of God. Their fate, too, is graphically depicted by Ezekiel (chapters 25–32), as they are by earlier prophets. These "prophecies against the nations" serve both to survey the known world, testifying to the prophet's visionary power, and to extend in space and time the comprehensive power of God to which the Israelites must attend if they are to be collectively sustained or restored and personally supported in the claim to righteousness.

The tonality of the prophets corresponds to the situations in which they find themselves. First Isaiah wrote as both Northern and Southern

Kingdoms were sustaining the threats and invasions of the vast, aggressive Assyrian Empire (740–701) and through the fall of the Northern Kingdom in 722. His utterances ring with immediate urgency. Second Isaiah has been discriminated as a separate prophet by commentators not just through specific historical references but through a change in tonality. He addresses himself to the threat of a distant and somewhat allegorized Babylon on a horizon that is taken to suggest the condition of exile. Third Isaiah buoyantly and expansively contemplates Israel's restoration from the Babylonian exile.

Over these cataclysmic centuries, the *habitus* of the Israelites is constantly jarred. When the exile comes, it has an internal as well as an external dimension: in the presence of suffering and defeat, they may respond either by self-purification or by corruption, and the situation both calls upon and empowers the prophet to recommend the course of virtue. The prophet's charisma is also personally dangerous because it is merely verbal. There is a congruence of the various prophets' roles with the variability of their historical foci, as these variously tighten the power relations of the language to which they have access. Since Ezekiel's king-in-exile has no power, the prophet is all but silent about him. A viable king only emerges in the late "David" run (37.24–28), with none of the three Isaiahs' recuperations into progressive historical stages. And Ezekiel has recourse, a dozen times in various contexts, to a weaker word than "king" to designate his leader, *nāś³î*, "chief," or "prince," a term that names the head of a smaller group with a less defined authority structure.[20]

For Ezekiel, the instabilities along the three interactive axes of the prophet-God-people triangle settles for a time into an ominous fixity once the second wave of exile has spent and Ezekiel finds himself by the banks of the Chebar. Paradoxically, this fixity in the spheres of power releases a fluidity in these interrelations, a fluidity coming forward in the variable distances of Ezekiel from his role and from his message. The first vision in the heavens culminates in the very symbol of power: at the top, a figure elevated upon a throne. But a large space of significative distance obtains between this image and the particular applications it might be given to the concrete situation to which it is ultimately addressed. "Above the firmament that was over their heads *was* the likeness of a throne, as the appearance of a sapphire stone; and upon the likeness of the throne *was* the likeness as the appearance of a man above upon it. . . . From the appearance of his loins even upward, and from the appearance of his loins even downward, I saw as it were the appearance of fire, and it had brightness round about. As the appearance of the bow that is in the cloud in the day of rain, so was the appearance of the brightness round about. This was the appearance of the glory of the Lord" (1.26–28). The glory of the Lord, his vivid brightness here, neither disappears nor unambiguously threatens the people, as does "the voice of one that spake" that concludes the passage. And the rainbow seems to promise rather than to warn, if its most distinct analogue be the Rainbow of the Covenant in Genesis 9.8–17. It is to be conceived of as connected to the restored Temple of the final vision, but this final vision, so extensive and detailed, is obscure as to its embodiment in any conceivably datable future. And this is the case when, for his present references, Ezekiel is so punctilious about dates.

The prophet always needs legitimation, and the legitimation on the vector prophet-people is subject to an instability inescapably derived from the unknowability of God's will in a specific situation. Such knowledge as there is has to come from the prophet himself, in a straining circularity.

One kind of language in Ezekiel, reminiscent of Deuteronomy in its summary repetitions, is sweeping, general, total, and abstract, presented in sequenced prose formulations that do not much resemble the admonitions of Isaiah and Jeremiah. For example, as God threatens the apocalyptic actions of pestilence, famine, and sword (5.12; 16–17), he lays out the general categories:

> Thus shall mine anger be accomplished, and I will cause my fury to rest upon them, and I will be comforted: and they shall know that I the Lord have spoken *it* in my zeal, when I have accomplished my fury in them. Moreover I will make thee waste, and a reproach among the nations that *are* round about thee, in the sight of all that pass by. So it shall be a reproach and a taunt, an instruction and an astonishment unto the nations that *are* round about thee, when I shall execute judgments in thee in anger and in fury and in furious rebukes. (5.13–15)

The same events, or the same sorts of events, keep coming into view, quite unlike the prophecy and the external situation in Jeremiah, which worsens progressively.

The visions themselves apply to the fate of Israel with greater or lesser specificity, constant changes of figuration, and intermittent abrupt reversal from woe to weal in both directions. Yet, curiously for such variation, Ezekiel is held responsible for warning the Israelites; and we can only deduce, since the application of the prophet's utterances often do not have such direct application, that not all of them can be interpreted without mediation as such warnings as the one the "watchman" is to deliver: "Son of man, I have made thee a watchman unto the house of Israel: therefore hear the word at my mouth, and warn them from me" (3.17–18). No clearer invocation could be imagined of the dynamic triangle God-prophet-people, but this closeness obtains of the surely intermittent, rather than constant, role of watchman. It is not always so evident in the relation between vision and event: "When I say unto the wicked, Thou shalt surely die; and thou givest him not warning, nor speakest to warn the wicked from his wicked way, to save his life; the same wicked *man* shall die in his iniquity; but his blood will I require at thine hand. Yet if thou warn the wicked, and he turn not then from his wickedness, nor from his wicked way, he shall die in his iniquity; but thou hast delivered thy soul" (3.18–19). The conditions evoked in this passage are emphatic, recursive, and locked in. They straighten their categories against the visions that considerably loosen them. Yet these categories help set up, as a flat analogy rather than as a historically grounded sequence, Egypt and Pharaoh. This analogy to Israel is two-pronged: the alternative is to resemble Pharaoh or to side with the failing Pharaoh in the vain hope of support—a contretemps that was already past, though of immediate memory, at the time of Ezekiel's writing.

After a characteristically precise indication of date near the climax of his address to the nations, the prophet is enjoined to speak to Pharaoh, but surely with the implication that his words will be heard mainly by the Israelites; he is, after all, speaking in Hebrew to begin with: "Son of man, speak unto Pharaoh king of Egypt, and to his multitude" (31.2). In eight verse strophes (31.3–10), there is first a metaphorical look at the comparative and successive stature of Egypt and

Assyria, with a retrospective matching prophecy about Assyria. Like the fall of the mighty Assyria for Egypt, it is implied, so will be the fall of the mighty Egypt for Israel—already a dual analogy. An extensive metaphor about a spreading lofty tree here depicts Assyria. This metaphor dwells so on superlatives that it calls Eden into the comparison (31.9; 31.18). All the more schematic then is the sudden reversal, represented by the text's switching from verse to prose: "I have driven him out for his wickedness" (31.11). The birds and the beasts who "dwelt in his shadow" (31.6) now dwell in the shadow of his ruin (31.13). The assertions, expanded throughout chapter 32, that all shall tremble at Egypt's fall carry only an oblique reference to Judah, since it is rolled together with other nations. Earlier, in chapter 20, where the Israelites' apostasy was equated with the prior apostasy in Egypt, the more direct comparison did not imply any deep recursion and transformation. Like a sort of overdetermination, chapter 32 picks up and dwells on an earlier Egypt-dragon metaphor, switching from the land out of which the prosperous tree grew, in the previous chapter, to a mention of seas, rivers, and waters.

There are, as Zimmerli argues, seventy-two occurrences of "proof-sayings" in Ezekiel. Their recurrence and multiplicity highlight the constancy of God's threat to the Israelites but also the instability of its application—and not only to themselves, since in many senses the analogy can be taken either way, but also between Israel and the dooms of Egypt and Assyria, Tyre and Babylon.

> This action, in which closer examination shows that Yahweh is always the subject, even when it is mentioned that his action is mediated by men, fulfills the function of a sign of proof that he is who he claims to be in his name. I have suggested the name "proof-saying" (*Erweiswort*) for this prophetic structure which appears so uncommonly frequently in Ezekiel. All the announcements of coming divine action, where they are couched in the recognition formula ["you will know that I am the Lord"], appear in the light of a divine self-evidencing. In his action in history Yahweh sets himself before his people and the world in his own person. All that which is preached by the prophet as an event which is apparently neutral in its meaning has its purpose in that Israel and the nations should come to a recognition, which in the

Old Testament always means an acknowledgement, of this person who reveals himself in his name. All Yahweh's action which the prophet proclaims serves as a proof of Yahweh among the nations.[21]

Over the whole book, such absolute utterances as that in 5.10, where son eats father and father eats son, must be taken not as final but as dire points in the unstable flow.[22] God holds them steadily and threateningly in view: "My eye will not be compassionate to you [*lō tāhôm ʿēnî ālayîk*]. Your abominations shall be in the midst of you" (7.4). Yet very soon, a somewhat more modified, though stern, admonition is offered: "Let not the buyer rejoice nor the seller mourn" (7.12). This is an apocalyptic, transeconomic view, superseded by another apocalypse in 7.13: "for the vision is touching the whole multitude." The tone for transmutation has been set at the start in the shift from the glory—and elaborate vision—at the end of chapter 1 to the conditions of woe at the beginning of chapter 2. This shift sets up a range in which even God, in the face of backsliding, can set up instability: "Because they had not executed my judgments . . . I gave them statutes that were not good" (20.24–25). And there is the puzzling statement in 22.29, which seems to put the prophet in harmony with a God who is silent: "Thus saith the Lord when the Lord God has not spoken." God declares, in 5.8–9, that he "will do in thee that which I have not done." A connection is broached in 11.22 between God's statements of eventual redemption (11.19–20) and the celestial movement of the cherubim and the wheels that was effectively set to stand over the whole book in the vision of the first chapter.

Overriding statements recur, as they do in the assertions—at once metalinguistic and metatheological—that come in 12.22–24: "Son of man, what *is* that proverb *that* ye have in the land of Israel, saying The days are prolonged and every vision faileth? Tell them therefore, thus saith the Lord God; I shall make this proverb to cease, and they shall no more use it as a proverb in Israel; but say unto them, The days are at hand, and the effect of every vision." (Here the intensive word for "vision," *ḥazon*, is used.) Two alternatives for prophetic protection are offered in negative form: "You have not gone into the gaps / or made a hedge" (13.5). God asks, "Why should I be inquired of this at all?"

(14.5). In saying this, he breaks the links in the vectors of his connection to prophet and people but only momentarily. There are looser, but stated, connections in the frequent recourse to the causal word *lemaan*, "wherefore," "because."

When Ezekiel employs the conventional metaphor of the whoredom of Israel (chapter 16), he offers a complicated history from birth to betrothal to God, then adduces multiple whoredoms that involve Assyria, Chaldea, and Egypt, with comparison (sister-daughter) to Samaria and Sodom—ending in a complex renewal of covenant/alienation of eternal covenant, *berît ʿôlām*. The faithless wife-harlot, along with her "sisters and daughters," is given a span from her birth as an abandoned foundling (16.5). A more elaborate series is offered for her here than in Hosea and Isaiah, with the grim addition of the human sacrifice of her children (16.36). And in chapter 23, the story of the two shameful women serves as an allegory for the two kingdoms, the vanished Northern Samaria, or Israel, and the recently conquered Southern Judah—a contrast picked up at 27.17 for climax and anticlimax when the two kingdoms, figured as faithless women, are called "merchants" for Tyre. More conventionally again, whoredoms repeated from the past are excoriated with simple verses (chapter 32). "I will consume thy filthiness out of thee" is mysteriously connected to "Thou shalt take thy inheritance" (22.15–16). "Thou shalt be filled with drunkenness and sorrow, with the cup of astonishment and desolation, with the cup of thy sister Samaria [the vanished Northern Kingdom]" (23.33). By 24.14–15, the city's lewdness will be burned away by fire.

In seeming contrast to the collective, public focus of prophecy generally, including his own, Ezekiel emphatically enunciates the principle of an individual guilt not historicized or collectivized into family or state (18.19). In this instance, the constant relation in developmental history of society to theology has seemed to be abrogated the more that this chapter goes on to set up emphatic corollaries. The repentant individual's sins are declared not to be remembered; nor are the backslider's virtues. This assertion is repeated like a litany, a sort of prose expansion of parallelism, which, in a sense, can pass away as it does because it has been dwelt on so fully and therefore, in some sense, expurgated. Chapter 33.12–16 repeats the importance of the final state of both the righteous and the sinner. The people are measured by three patriarchs of "righteousness," *ṣedaqāh*, who are too remote in time and space to be included in developmental history: "Though ... Noah, Daniel [not the prophet], and Job, were in it, they should deliver but their own souls by their righteousness" (14.14).

David will be king "forever" (37.25). He must be a metaphorical David, like the Jacob soon mentioned, "one shepherd" (37.24), in the reversion to that metaphor.[23] "One king for all" (37.22) is not derivable from the sticks of the dry bones prophecy in this chapter. The answer of God simply continues, "neither shall they be divided into two kingdoms any more at all," harking back over two centuries to the division of the kingdom, in Ezekiel's often abrupt, momentary, and seemingly discordant reference to earlier history.[24]

As the book moves towards the vision of the Temple, enemies are brought in again, this time the Gog and Magog of chapters 38 and 39, who seem to be a collective cover name for all enemies. Then the long Temple vision rounds out the prophecy, introduced and carried out by an intermediary between God and the prophet, a man who is also effectually an "interpreting angel," as Zimmerli says: "In the man of ch 40ff the *angelus interpres* is undoubtedly prefigured, who then appears as a firmly defined figure in the night-visions of Zechariah."[25] Here, however, the figure cannot be so pinned down but only correlated loosely with the man of the first vision and its varied repetitions in chapters 8–11. Ezekiel's presentation here sets the wide, celestial frame for the future-orientation of the long Temple vision: "[God] set me upon a very high mountain, by which *was* as the frame of a city on the south" (40.2).

In some ways, this final Temple vision touches on the first vision, but in other ways, it is completely new, offering a bird's-eye view of lands and heaven out beyond its gates. In the effect of its elaborate and precise measurements, this vision qualifies and transforms the elaborate and precise measurements of Solomon's Temple. The man of brass (or bronze) with a line of flax and a measuring reed, as he shows the Temple, mainly points towards its visual attributes. After the prophet has been taken to what seem the final measurements outside the Temple, an area five hundred reeds square (42.15–20), he is sud-

denly shown a superseding vision: "behold, the glory of the God of Israel came from the way of the east: and his voice *was* like the noise of
many waters: and the earth shined with his glory" (43.2). Now he links
it to his first vision, using the same terminology: "And *it was* according
to the appearance of the vision which I saw, *even* according to the vision
that I saw when I came to destroy the city" (43.3). The term "destroy"
here foreshortens the complex process by which, after the incipient fall
of the city, the prophet transmits God's warning that he will visit further punishments upon the people. Now, in a foreshortening of time
into space, the complete restoration of the city is envisioned around this
Temple. It is indicated by God as "the place of my throne, and the place
of the soles of my feet, where I will dwell in the midst of the children of
Israel for ever. . . . Show the house to the house of Israel . . . and let them
measure the pattern" (43.7–10). "The law of the house" is established,
including sacrifice procedures (43.18; 45.18), like those in Leviticus.

By chapter 45, the focus of the Temple enlarges gradually to include
the whole country. The magnified outer measure has now become
twenty-five thousand by ten thousand reeds, and in a further extension
beyond even that measure, Ezekiel is shown trees at the brink of the
river, running from the east country and down through the desert
to the sea. Soon the borders of the land will be measured through the
whole country (47.13–22). The survey in chapter 48 comprises twelve
tribes and territories, and in 48.31, the gates are successively named for
them. Here naming functions as a global and permanent reconstitution
of the people, as well as a recapitulation. The whole book thus ends
with the geographical and optical survey of the land and the gates of
the city. It closes with the much longer consideration of a real but still
future space on a redeemed earth. The space of the new land counterbalances and fulfills the initial balance in the opening heaven that had
been vouchsafed to this mighty speaker.

It is space that predominates here under a millennial time, rather
than the powerful proximate time of the earlier prophets, with its op-
erative past and tensing future. Ezekiel has, at it were, substituted
space for time in this last vision, which extends the Temple outward
from more usual measurements into an extent that encompasses the
whole space of his lost country. The vision fills its extent horizontally,

just as the first vision had filled its space vertically, all the way up to the firmament and then to the throne above it. In the vertical vision, the heavens predominate; in the horizontal one, the earth. But they fold into each other and mass together, as do the bones in the valley where God had the prophet resurrect them.

5

Sign, Song, and Prayer in the Dynamic Internality of Psalms

IN PSALMS, the prophet drops out as an intermediary and the elements of discourse undergo a shift. "The people" directly address God, even if the formation of this or that particular psalm is attributed to some traditional author, notably the prophetic figure David. And even if a first person is used, it must be construed as a collective first person under an associative conception of the psalms taken together in their literary form—as well as in the immemorial use of the Psalter for the communal recitation of worship. "*There is* no more any prophet [for us]"—this statement, which comes forward in the fluid process of one psalm (74.9), is a statement impossible in prophecy itself.

When a psalm speaks of transgressions, it tends to be with contrition rather than with a prophet's warning in view. And when it speaks of joy, it tends to celebrate rather than to promise. Typically and pervasively, the psalms speak of direct interaction between God and people, as in this run, which recalls the possibility of bounty even as it recounts punishment for apostasy:

> I *am* the Lord thy God
> Which brought thee out of the land of Egypt:
> Open thy mouth wide, and I will fill it.
> But my people would not hearken to my voice;
> And Israel would none of me.
> So I gave them up unto their own hearts' lust:
> *And* they walked in their own counsels.
> Oh that my people had hearkened unto me,
> *And* Israel had walked in my ways!
> I should soon have subdued their enemies,
> And turned my hand against their adversaries.
> The haters of the Lord should have submitted themselves unto him:

But their time should have endured for ever.
He should have fed them also with the finest of the wheat:
And with honey out of the rock should I have satisfied thee.

(81.10–16)

The alternatives of holy and unholy behavior and their matching consequences are presented as in the prophets but without the injunction of the prophets and without an adaptive sequence of time. This same psalm begins "Sing aloud unto God our strength, / Make a joyful noise unto the God of Jacob" (81.1). It swings away from, but also back toward, celebration, bolstering itself with a certain confidence that God can be quoted, again without the intermediation of a prophet. So the psalms tend to assert a certain security:

If they break my statutes,
And keep not my commandments;
Then will I visit their transgression with the rod,
And their iniquity with stripes.
Nevertheless my loving-kindness will I not utterly take from him,
Nor suffer my faithfulness to fail.
My covenant will I not break,
Nor alter the thing that is gone out of my lips.
Once have I sworn by my holiness
That I will not lie unto David.

(89.31–35)

In the view presented by these lines, there is no avoiding the certainty of punishment; but loving-kindness remains, with a certitude not promised in any of the prophets, and it remains even in the face of a general condition of distress elaborated in a later run of the same psalm (89.48–50).

Psalm 2 sets up a general pattern for kings and a static contrast of supersession and derision on the part of God. This register of assertions differs deeply from the adaptive, historically oriented dynamism of the prophets:

The kings of the earth set themselves,
And the rulers take counsel together,
Against the Lord, and against his Anointed, *saying*
Let us break their bands asunder,

And cast away their cords from us.
He that sitteth in the heavens shall laugh:
The Lord shall have them in derision.

(2.2–4)

The command "do my prophets no harm" (105.15) comes in another re-run of highlights from the pre-Exodus and Exodus narratives. The effect of this command is to set the prophets up as a permanent body under a group of permanent conditions that here find articulation through and toward the people.

In Psalms, the dimensionalized time-reach of the prophets is redeployed into a feeling that is dynamized and often internalized. This process tends ultimately to feed a long past into a confident joy rather than into lament. The time is general and unspecified in "What work thou did in their days, / in the times of old" (44.1). Time here serves not as the unfolding nucleus of charged testing and promised fulfillment, as it does in the prophets, but as a comforting base for the dynamic feeling of the speaker. A permanent condition is envisaged throughout. And even when God is set against sinners, recuperation is felt to be close at hand without the stressful collective action enjoined by the prophets. The many references to the Exodus tend to treat that sequence of events as a fixed point, seen as the result of an abiding condition:

He turned the sea into dry *land*:
They went through the flood on foot:
There did we rejoice in him.
He ruleth by his power for ever.

(66.6–7)

These references to the Exodus, however detailed they become, do not function as warnings and do not envisage a linkage to a causal series. The long account in Psalm 78 offers a recapitulation of the plagues of Egypt, an account that memorializes and celebrates as it recapitulates. Of Moses and Aaron, it is asserted, "Thou wast a God that forgavest them, / Though thou tookest vengeance of their inventions" (99.8). A run reminiscent of Jacob's deathbed blessing is given in Psalm 108.7–14 and serves again as a celebratory reminder. And this run is also a repetition, weaving together passages from other psalms (namely, 57.8–12 with 60.6–12). The psychospiritual effects of the return from Babylon are characterized as a simple spiritual condition: "They that sow in tears / Shall reap in joy" (126.5). Psalm 136 is built upon the refrain "For his mercy [*ḥesed*] *endureth* forever," repeated in every other verse. It compasses and casts into permanent exempla a vast range of events from the Creation on, verses 5–9 recapitulating Genesis 1.14–16. The time in view sets the language of a psalm into accord with God's millennial reach: "the word *which* he commanded a thousand generations" (105.8). The celebratory tone can always expand with seeming ease into this long view:

> Lord, thou hast been our dwelling place in all generations.
> Before the mountains were brought forth,
> Or ever thou hadst formed the earth and the world,
> Even from everlasting to everlasting, thou *art* God.
> Thou turnest man to destruction [or "contrition"];
> And sayest, Return, ye children of men.
> For a thousand years in thy sight
> *Are but* as yesterday when it is past,
> And *as* a watch in the night.
> Thou carriest them away as with a flood; they are *as* a sleep:
> In the morning *they are* like grass *which* groweth up.
> In the morning it flourisheth, and groweth up;
> In the evening it is cut down, and withereth.
> For we are consumed by thine anger,
> And by thy wrath are we troubled.
> Thou hast set our iniquities before thee,
> Our secret *sins* in the light of thy countenance.
> For all our days are passed away in thy wrath:
> We spend our years as a tale *that is told*.
>
> (90.1–9)

The basic assumption here associates the life cycle of human beings to the cycle of the seasons and also to the vast millennial progression of a time of which God is master. Inside the fundament of assumption and in the coordinates such utterance assumes, the iniquities of humankind and God's corresponding anger are, in a sense, masterable because they are inevitable. Instead of being subjected to the deep turmoil of a sin-perverted national periodization, as is true in the prophets, human behavior, under the force of such prayers, can be envisioned as moving once again into a relationship of loving-kindness. There is expectation of a favorable response in the injunction toward the end of this same psalm, "Let thy work appear unto thy servants, / And thy glory unto their children" (90.16). "Nevertheless he saved them for his name's sake" (106.8), it is said of God's response to the iniquity of the Israelites at the time of the Exodus. Here God is kind in spite of humankind's rebellious behavior, a dynamic that is alien to that expressed by the prophets. And as this psalm progresses (106.27–42), God changes from punishing the Israelites to restoring them to righteousness: "Many times did he deliver them" (106.43). On the other hand, it is as though exact retribution were taken for granted, while at the same time the application of God's favor and disfavor is arbitrarily defined even within the scope of a single psalm, such as Psalm 107:

> He turneth rivers into a wilderness,
> . . . A fruitful land into barrenness,
> For the wickedness of them that dwell therein.

> (107.33–34)

And then the process is reversed and reversed again (107.35–42), without an explicit matching of human behavior to God's favor. Mystery and majesty are assumed, somewhat as they are in Job, but without strenuousness and stress: "Whoso *is* wise, and will observe these *things*, / Even they shall understand the loving-kindness of the Lord" (107.43). Thus this psalm concludes. The vantage of a general blessedness in the tie between God and the individual soul, as figured in and through the people, persists for assertion in runs such as those of Psalms 121–129. The recompense of a general good for good actions is felt to persist against the recompense of evil for evil. At one extreme of the mystery are statements such as "If thou, Lord, shouldest mark iniquities, / O Lord, who shall stand?" (130.3). The statement envisions a permanent, ongoing propensity for sin, much like the Christian one. Yet resolution comes at once: "But *there is* forgiveness with thee" (130.4). And by the end of the psalm "he shall redeem Israel / From all his iniquities." As happens in Psalm 142, there is a constant and loose, if sometimes ominously correspondent, interaction between God's favor to the speaker and the speaker's righteousness. "Put not your trust in princes / *Nor* in the son of man" (146.3) implies a permanent condition at once of threatening iniquity and countervailing divine favor. "Of [also "in," or "with"] thy mercy [*ḥesed*] cut off my enemies" (143.12) shows that the attribute usually characterized as "loving-kindness" or "graciousness" extends even to extermination. "The Lord *is* righteous in all his ways, / And holy [*ḥāsîd*] in all his works" (145.17). God is spoken of earlier in this psalm with the same term, comprised in the formulas from Deuteronomy, "The Lord *is* gracious, and full of compassion; / Slow to anger, and of great mercy [*ḥesed*]" (145.8). "The time to favor her, yea, the set time, is come" (102.13) gives no sense of historical development in the manner of the prophets. Through vast time "thou *art* the same / And thy years shall have no end" (102.27).

The template of the genus *psalm* provides not a structure but a permissible range of effusions delineating feelings and a free flow for them from visionary hope to visionary despair within the same strophic run. A grounded trust in God's accessibility to the voice of the people sanctions the leap from "My God, my God, why hast thou forsaken me" (22.1) to "The Lord *is* my shepherd; I shall not want" (23.1). This leap can often be matched in the fluid adaptability of spiritual mood within many single psalms, including Psalm 22 itself, where the turn comes in a single verse from the initial run of despair (22.1–20), ending in "Save me from the lion's mouth" (22.21), taken over for a run of confident praise (22.22–31) that begins "For thou hast heard me from the horns of the unicorns [or "wild oxen"]" (22.21). The cover of collectivity gathers up the momentary feeling, within an individual line or a whole psalm, and makes it always true, presumptively or actually, of an "I." The primacy of a feeling that is presumed to be connected to God, who is conceived of as a constant auditor, licenses the fusion of the singular into the collective plural.

"My tongue is the pen of a ready writer" (45.1) appears in a psalm that turns out to be a marriage song. The psalm illustrates what seems superficially to be the miscellaneous nature of the collection by ranging through military preparedness, the prowess of the king who is to be married, and the steady-state conception of social life that is exhibited by the psalms generally, even when some of them happen to reflect a particular political situation. The public circumstance is typically generalized, as compared to that in the prophets, even when it is set into a long-range, mutating dynamic of this "song of loves," *šir yedhidhoth*, as this psalm is characterized in the headnote. Terms for song—*šir, zamir, mizmor*—come up all the time and are also used to characterize these "praise songs," *tehīllîm*, which is translated by the Greek term "psalm."

Song, in Lévi-Strauss's anthropological emphasis, is continuous, where speech is discontinuous.[1] In music, even the silences are reckoned into the rhythmic counting, and this book of songs implies a music, even through the silences of the break from psalm to psalm. The music posits a continuity of utterance in which the fullness of expression stands available for an implied totalization. A perfection may always merge into an utterance, and after the lament of Psalm 17 and the restoration of Psalm 18 comes the "new song" of Psalm 19:[2]

> The heavens declare the glory of God;
> And the firmament showeth his handiwork.
> Day unto day uttereth speech,
> And night unto night showest knowledge.
> *There is* no speech nor language,
> *Where* their voice is not heard.
> Their line is gone out through all the earth,
> And their words to the end of the world.
> In them hath he set a tabernacle for the sun,
> Which *is* as a bridegroom coming out of his chamber,
> *And* rejoiceth as a strong man to run a race.
> His going forth *is* from the end of the heaven,
> And his circuit unto the ends of it:
> And there is nothing hid from the heat thereof.
>
> (19.1–7)

As God overmasters the old Sun God, he integrates with the temple, with the bridegroom as a strong man in his fertile social function, and with the whole firmament. A speechless knowledge and a silent language have found their way into the psalm's language of praise: "*There is* no speech nor language." "New song" is the term of Psalm 96:

> O sing unto the Lord a new song:
> Sing unto the Lord, all the earth.
> Sing unto the Lord, bless his name;

Show forth his salvation from day to day.
Declare his glory among the heathen,
His wonders among all people.

(96.1–3)

This text, with small variations, is ascribed to David in Chronicles 16.23–33. The psalm is so general that is has been taken to mean both a return from exile and a messianic restoration of Jehovah.[3] And psalms draw on their fundament with an implied assumption of such concord that they do not exclude repetitions, partial and whole. Psalms 14 and 53 are the same psalm, and Psalms 17 and 18 in turn overlap with 2 Samuel 22.

"Hold not thy peace, O God of my praise" (109.2). This expression anchors in the conception of utterance here, in an evoked reply that could be not just words but a speaking action. The rest of the psalm implies as much, even though the formal statement "hold not thy peace" (literally, "be not silent," *ᶜal teḥereš*) refers to withheld speech. "Thou hast magnified thy words above all thy name" (138.2) extends the principle of full utterance over the principle of God's full action in an excess of expression that simultaneously states an equation at the limits of speech. There is a sort of double excess, in both directions, word and action, that comes to an equality. To be sure, the "words" here can be glossed "promises." Yet the term used is not *dāvār*, "word," or "thing," but *imrāh*, "saying." All the more, then, does the primary lexical sense indicate "words," which must be subcategorized as "promises" to bring this exuberance within range.[4]

"They have set up their ensigns *for* signs" (74.4) literally means "They have set up their signs of signs," *šāmû ᵓôtōtām ᵓōtôt*. As the psalm continues, the "signs of signs" interact with and go under to the "name" of God. In the face of these enemies "We see not our signs / *There is* no more any prophet" (74.19). Yet the very reach of the utterance here implies, as the psalm goes on, that the speakers whose chosenness is exemplified in their access to this utterance will in fact be restored, since the name of God is superior to, as well as inclusive of, all signs.

The exuberance of the language of such song leads to a dimensionalizing of metaphor:

> Lead me to the rock *that* is higher than I.
> For thou hast been a shelter for me,
> *And* a strong tower from the enemy.
>
> (61.2–3)

The breadth of reference here does not exclude a literal tower or a literal shelter comprised in the common metaphor of "rock," whose suggestions of a cliff may also include reference to the existence of natural defenses in a place like the Holy Land. And this possibility is even more powerfully and specifically probable because, as Othmar Keel has demonstrated, the Psalms deal fluidly, extensively, and specifically with a large repository of images found in Near Eastern visual representations and traditions. The cliff is not only a type of defense but a specific feature of the site of Jerusalem.[5]

Jerusalem itself all along serves metaphorically as well as literally, notably in Psalm 48. "My goodness [*ḥesed*] and my fortress" (144.2), spoken about God, brings qualities and concrete (metaphorical) entities into a single vision. The creation expands in the referential sweep of such utterance:

> Bless the Lord, O my soul.
> O Lord my God, thou art very great;
> Thou art clothed with honor and majesty:
> Who coverest *thyself* with light as *with* a garment:
> Who stretchest out the heavens like a curtain:
> Who layeth the beams of his chambers in the waters:
> Who maketh the clouds his chariot:
> Who walketh upon the wings of the wind:
> Who maketh his angels spirits;
> His ministers a flaming fire:
> *Who* laid the foundations of the earth,
> *That* it should not be removed for ever.
> Thou coverest it with the deep as *with* a garment:
> The waters stood above the mountains.
>
> (104.1–6)

Each feature here reshapes staples of Near Eastern cosmological representation, such as the relation of earth, water, and heaven found, for example, on Egyptian sarcophagi—the clothing, the curtains, the foundations, the chariot, the wings, and the mountains. Further, there is a mastering millennial continuity and a kind of daring sweep involved in stretching the heavens like a curtain, laying the beams of chambers in the waters, making the clouds a chariot, and walking on the wings of the wind. Here fluidity buckles before mastery, the more that the staple images govern and focus the representation, while continuing the paradox of the waters standing above the mountains. The waters are also a garment; in this run, the staircase parallelism keeps the garment as the constant feature of reference: the garment clothes creation, but God himself is also clothed; his being clothed with honor and majesty is an aspect of the greatness of his being, and it gears itself with a Near Eastern image of the clothing of the king.[6] This psalm extends the note of praise, and praise here entails and empowers an assimilative recapitulation of majestic attributes and forces. All this play of traditional image becomes, through utterance, an internalization of the collective speaker's focused prayerfulness and an externalization of it out to the largest constituents of space and time.

The dimension of time becomes apparent as the psalm continues. In this whole psalm, also, Genesis is replayed as a deepening and refashioning of the particularities in creation, as a nonnarrative presentness. The praise of Creation in Psalms echoes Job but without the intermediation of dramatic confrontation. As it reaches the end, this psalm makes the praise explicit:

> I will sing unto the Lord as long as I live.
> I will sing praise to my God while I have my being.
> My meditation of him shall be sweet.

(104.33–34)

"Be sweet," *ᶜarav*, implies sacrifice, as the Soncino commentary spells out.[7] The force of "meditation," *śiḥi*, implies anxiety and complaint, as well as musing and speech; all utterance, even a stressful mood, is caught up in the overriding splendor. In "My foot standeth in an even place. / In the congregation will I bless the Lord" (26.12), the conventional metaphor "foot" is here enlivened to suggest the integration of the whole society. "Thou hast set my feet in a broad room" (31.9) praises what it envisions. A comparable verbal intensification operates on terms like "enemy," "rescue," "rock", and especially "battle," which, both alone and in conjunction with other elements, is often found in Psalms. The same intensification of reference happens with notions like "the help of my countenance" and the metaphors of "face," "pit," and "cut off," among others. "Let them be as grass *upon* the housetops / which withereth afore it groweth up" (129.6) is a complex spatial image that merges the population of defective worshippers into the processes of the nature controlled by God.

All this sweep of reference is achieved through an intensification of language that tends to seem more diluted in translation. The half-lines are generally formed of runs of three- or four-word kernels, which are not spaced apart the way they appear in translation. So, for example, in the passage quoted above, Psalm 19.1–7, each line is only three or four words long. The line "Which *is* as a bridegroom coming out of his chamber" (19.6) has just four words, *vehû> kehātān yōṣe> mēḥûpetô*; the line "And there is nothing hid from the heat thereof" (19.7) has just three, *ve>ēn nīstār mēḥammatô*.[8] To take another example from the elaborate alphabet of Psalm 119, verse 88 consists of only two words, *keḥasdekā ḥayēnî* [literally, "As thy loving-kindness (or "mercy") quicken me"], and the intensification produced by having its senses packed into just these two is furthered by the spread of repetitions through this longest of the psalms. These two words conjoin again in verses 149 and 159, after appearing in other combinations elsewhere, the first word appearing twice, the second seven times. The repetitions of words are constant, the variations among the repetitions manifold, fortifying the formal repetition of sense that is entailed in the verse parallelism.

In alphabet psalms like Psalms 111 and 127 and especially Psalm 119, an extra, arbitrary "literary" pattern of an obligatory progress through the alphabet is added to the elaborate weave of verbal repetitions. The formality to which this draws is loosely implicit in the recursions and repetitions of the form and in the associative freedom of all psalms, with their template of possible connections that are actualized from a staple of interconnected devotional terms. The fact that each verse begins with the same letter of the alphabet regularizes and severely contains each into an alliterative anaphora. So, for example, in

Psalm 119, verses 81 and 82 add to these devices the near echo of near rhyme, *kaltā/kālû*, picked up in verse 86, *kāl*. The anaphora is matched by nearly acrostic repetition and all within the frame of the alphabet, an arbitrary reference to elements of language. Here are the verses of the last stanza, the *tāw* stanza:

> Let my cry come near before thee, O Lord:
> Give me understanding according to thy *word.
> Let my supplication come before thee:
> Deliver me according to thy *word.
> My lips shall utter praise,
> When thou hast taught me thy *statutes.
> My tongue shall speak of thy word:
> For all thy *commandments *are* righteousness.
> Let thine hand help me;
> For I have chosen thy *precepts.
> I have longed for thy salvation, O Lord;
> And thy *law *is* my delight.
> Let my soul live, and it shall praise thee;
> And let thy *judgments help me.
> I have gone astray like a lost sheep: seek thy servant;
> For I do not forget thy *commandments.
>
> (119.169–76)

As a kind of counterpart to the rigid pattern in which every pair of verses begins with the same letter, in this case *tāw*, every one of the twenty-two stanzas of Psalm 119, as Charles A. Briggs points out, repeats with variation the repertoire of eight terms for the law: (1) *dāvār*, "word" or "thing"; (2) *īmrāh*, "saying"; (3) *ḥûqqîm*, "statutes"; (4) *miš-paṭîm*, "judgments"; (5) *torah*, "law"; (6) *ᶜedôt*, "testimonies"; (7) *miṣvôt*, "commandments"; (8) *peqqûdîm*, "precepts."[9] In the *tāw* stanza above, the English equivalents for these terms, when they occur, are marked with asterisks. (It should be noted that both *dāvār* and *īmrāh* are translated "word.") Coming almost schematically in every other line of the stanza, the terms constitute a reticulation, matching semantically the sound pattern of the initial *tāw*, which comes also once every other line. But beyond this pattern of faithful repetition of the words for "law" in each of the twenty-two stanzas, in this final stanza there is a heavy repetition of terms that occur within this one psalm and all the more so from psalm to psalm. Just about every other expression in this stanza is repeated within the psalm, some of them many times.[10]

The conception of an address from the people to God energizes these repetitions and funds them in an utterance of which the intensities are cumulative. This rigorously controlled psalm, like many others, does not reach for inventive ornament, because the terms, ordered and repeated, carry and reverberate the devotional posture they assume through the utterance. Noteworthy descriptions or flourishes are not necessarily present, as can be seen in the apparent flatness of this concluding strophe. As this psalm says a little earlier, "The entrance of thy words giveth light" (119.130), literally, "the opening of your words lightens," a statement that expresses the way the psalm envisions the ritual thrust and spiritual function of its own language: "But I give myself unto prayer" (109.4), or literally, "I am [all] prayer," *ʾanî tefillāh.* There is envisioned a full encompassing anywhere of the speaker by God, a notion especially clear in 139.10–16, where it is asserted that "in thy book all *my members* were written" (139.16). This feeling in its scope can startlingly include primitive hostility, as in the expressed wish to dash the heads of enemy infants against a rock (137.9). It also includes the extreme acceptance of penitential suffering, "Let the righteous smite me; *it shall be* a kindness" (141.5). Were it not for the grounding in the deep context of the utterance to which a long tradition of spiritual commentary attests,[11] a psalm's range of expressions would seem random and miscellaneous, as they do even in this lucid and balanced description by S. R. Driver:

> The Psalms, speaking generally, consist of reflexions, cast into a poetical form, upon the various aspects in which God manifests Himself either in nature, or towards Israel, or the individual soul, accompanied often—or, indeed, usually—by an outpouring of the emotions and affections of the Psalmist, prompted by the warmth of his devotion to God, though varying naturally in character, according to the circumstances in which he is placed. Thus, in some Psalms the tone is that of praise or thanksgiving, in others it is one of penitence or supplication, in others again it is meditative or didactic: not unfrequently also a Psalm is of mixed character; it begins, perhaps, in a strain of supplication, and as the poet pro-

ceeds the confidence that his prayer will be answered grows upon him in a tone of jubilant exultation (e.g. Pss. 6, 13, 22, . . . 26, 31, 36, 64, 69, 71). In the Psalter the *devotional* element of the religious character finds its completest expression; and the soul is displayed in converse with God, disclosing to Him in manifold emotions, desires, aspirations, or fears.[12]

Put differently, the utterance does not build to a revelation, though along the way it can include expressions of revelatory force. Rather, the utterance comes into the musical continuity of its song by following a thread of psychospiritual self-characterization ranging from despair to joy and from lament to confident exuberance, always arcing back and forth and keyed to praise of God: "My heart and my flesh crieth out for the living God" (84.2). Here the verb "cry out," *rānan*, is intensive and implicitly musical, a "ringing cry of joy"; "Out of the *depths* [of water] have I cried unto thee" (130.1). These songs can move into and out of refrain—and parallelism is itself a kind of varied refrain—but unevenly, as though responding to the power of the devotional act that they constitute. "Cause thy face to shine and we shall be saved," *vehaēr panēka venîvašʿeāh* (80.3), is repeated at 80.8 and again at 80.19. In "The Lord God *is* a sun and shield" (84.11), the secure joy carries right through; the judgment and the strength imply the possibility of other forces, sometimes cosmic ones. These are picked up again in 97.4–5:

> His lightnings enlightened the world:
> The earth saw, and trembled.
> The hills melted like wax at the presence of the Lord.

The psychospiritual response is correspondingly comprehensive: "Light is sown for the righteous / And gladness for the upright in heart" (97.11). And the psychological inwardness affects all. So a psalm may declare its own action: "Declare [or "number"] his works with rejoicing" (107. 22)—an injunction followed by the next verses. "Then shall the wicked see *it* and be grieved / He shall gnash his teeth and melt away" (112.10).

In Psalm 60, God both oppresses and exalts his people, as against other peoples such as Moab and Philistia. This interaction is expressed without any invocation of the prophet-people-God triangle of reciprocities, although Psalm 69, "I am come unto the deep waters" (69.2), recalls the Jeremiah register throughout. Yet the difference will assert itself at the end when the expression is divorced from the prophet's exemplary person. Nor is a psalm bound by the keynote of Lamentations, which it may leave as freely as it may enter. The joy of piety persistently supervenes: "My soul *is* even as a weaned child" (131.2). And intensification stands to prompt the voice of the speaker: "Let thy priests be clothed with righteousness [*ṣedeq*]; / And let thy saints [*ḥasîdeka*] shout for joy" (132.9); and the intensive "shout aloud for joy" is repeated at 132.16. "Let the saints be joyful in glory: / Let them sing aloud upon their beds" (149.5) supposedly implies a sleep safe of enemies, but it does so by extending to every activity of life the activity that the psalms praise and engage in. The image of the singing sleeper in this line would be nearly surrealistic, if it were not based upon a sense of every activity as a worshipful utterance when seen and expressed in the light of an actual utterance wholly grounded in worship.

In such worship and joy do the Psalms conclude. The last line of all, "Let every thing that hath breath praise the Lord / Praise ye the Lord" (150.6), simply produces a near repetition in its final word, *halelûyāh*. It exuberantly simplifies and reverses the parallel, repeated term "Haleluhuh" coming first shortly in every verse of this psalm, keeping the praise explicit in these songs of praise.

6

Self-Reference, Prophetic Recursion, and Image in Ecclesiastes

THE FIRST WORDS of Ecclesiastes indicate the metamorphosis that the prophetic tradition has undergone through the centralization of the wisdom tradition. Indeed, more than any other wisdom text, Ecclesiastes fixes its fusion of roles from the start: "The words of the Preacher [*qôhelet*, "convener"], son of David, king in Jerusalem" (1.1). The action of the prophet, to call the people together and speak, and the message of the prophet are linked to a legendary wise king, Solomon, here defined in terms of his descent from David, a king who was also a prophet. The vision of empire and career and life cycle in this book distantly echoes the themes of prophecy, while at the same time enlisting the parallelism of biblical poetry in new ways. The wisdom tradition of Proverbs, sometimes continuous in its runs, has been adapted in Ecclesiastes to a new rhythmic continuity in which the skillfully modulated flow, allowing for prose punctuations, appears in sharp relief, especially if it is seen in the light of the similar, longer, but somewhat more simply additive Ecclesiasticus. A comparison with The Wisdom of Solomon, too, will point up how integrally shaped Ecclesiastes is.

In the suppleness of this flow, contradictions as well as varied repetitions and qualifications are absorbed into the overall harmony, which manages to string together proverbs without either obscuring their distinct, aphoristic force or allowing them to come apart disjunctively:

Vanity of vanity, saith the Preacher,
Vanity of vanities; all is vanity.
What profit hath a man of all his labor
Which he taketh under the sun?
One generation passeth away, and *another* generation cometh:
But the earth abideth forever.
The sun also ariseth and the sun goeth down,
And hasteth to his place where he arose.

The wind goeth toward the south,
And turneth about unto the north;
It whirleth about continually,
And the wind returneth again according to his circuits.
All the rivers run into the sea,
Yet the sea is not full;
Unto the place from whence the rivers come,
Thither they return again.
All things *are* full of labor;
Man cannot utter *it*:
The eye is not satisfied with seeing,
Nor the ear filled with hearing.
The thing that hath been,
It *is that* which shall be;
And that which is done *is* that which shall be done:
And *there is* no new *thing* under the sun.

(1.2–9)

The thematic control and poise are evident from the very first, and the tone is rich and emphatic. This tone blends the prophetic long view and a new pattern of privacy that merges a view of natural process with a moral posture some have found reminiscent of the Epicureans, in a spirit of resignation some have heard as an echo of the Stoics.

However, a comparison to formal Greek and Roman Epicureanism, Stoicism, and Scepticism highlights the crucial differences between the Greek and Hebrew traditions and serves to demonstrate the strong contextual permeation of a social situs in this text.[1] The Hebrew wise man, the *ḥākām*, is at the center of the society, a spokesman for its wisdom and, putatively, all the more so when he has cast himself in the role of a king of legendary power and legendary wisdom. The Stoic or Epicurean, by contrast, is a professional philosopher tending to the margins of society, even in less extreme cases than the vagabond Diogenes or the slave Epictetus. Ecclesiastes has relations to a literary tradition and a social history, as well as norms he follows even as he transmutes them. This writer looks to the past and not just to the philosopher's future. The future the "preacher" sees, too, is closer in tone to the prophet's than to the philosopher's. From these opening words on, there is nothing in Ecclesiastes that cannot be adaptively correlated to the realistic long view of the prophets or the homely practicality of Proverbs. The Greek philosopher, on the other hand, has a relation to, and takes his bearings from, a tradition of argument and cross-questioning. He responds to puzzles, whereas Ecclesiastes articulates a wisdom from the depth. Epicurus and the Stoa recommend exercises for the future; Ecclesiastes offers a yield from the past. "*There is* no remembrance of the wise more than of the fool for ever" (2.16). Such a lack of remembrance, among many other ideas in this book, is not Greek. "I have said in mine heart, Go to now, I will prove thee with mirth, therefore enjoy pleasure: and behold, this also is vanity" (2.3). Quite apart from the pregnant paradox built into this verse and spread through the whole of Ecclesiastes, only the injunction to enjoy pleasure has the ring of Epicurus, and even that provides nothing like his integral analysis; it is proverbial rather than philosophical. The notion "prove thee with mirth" is transprophetic, putting the trials of the people by God into an extreme form, while "this also is vanity" sees transience not in either a physiological Epicurean sense nor a moral Stoic one—and still less in a Skeptical light. It, too, is by and large proverbial. A later (and subliminally parallel) expression in the chapter also mingles resignation and a deep piety more in harmony with Amos than with any Greek philosopher:

> *There is* nothing better for a man, *than* that he should eat and drink, and *that* he should make his soul enjoy good in his labor. This also I saw, that it *was* from the hand of God. For who can eat, or who else can hasten *hereunto*, more than I? For God giveth to a man that *is* good in his sight, wisdom, and knowledge, and joy: but to the sinner he giveth travail, to gather and to heap up, that he may give to *him that is* good before God. This also *is* vanity and vexation of spirit. (2.24–26)

Here the arresting conjunction of "joy" with "wisdom" and "knowledge" internalizes the prosperity that accompanies virtue in the prophets and evens out what the prophet possesses, "wisdom" and "knowledge," with what any person may have access to.

In the light of what is said throughout the book, the speaker's self-identification as Solomon is a dramatic posture providing a vantage for him, a sort of megaphone through which he may speak to those he has "convened." The dramatization of the persona is powerful and original;

it would be inconceivable for a prophet to so impersonate a ruler. Pretending to be a king, historicized and legendary, provides a template that can address the past from an ideal elevation; he remains private and can emphasize his personal triumphs to the exclusion of public worries—and yet he can draw on the permanent, public legacy to the people in the Temple with which both kings are associated. As de Vaux says, "David first thought of having a Temple and . . . Solomon actually built it."[2] This achievement is surely referred to, but from an oblique and private angle, when the speaker says, "I made me great works," *hīgdaltî ma'aśai*; literally, "I magnified my works" (2.4). He then goes on to list activities of self-enrichment for arranging the large house, vineyards, parks, ponds, servants, and male and female singers, all organized for various, essentially private, pleasures. This is a villa-like king's existence. Nothing is said about public activities or the religious activities on which the Temple centered; in this respect, Ecclesiastes departs from the account of Solomon and other rulers in the Books of Kings, though in many respects the accounts there are followed.[3] Nor is there any reference here to the military activities that preoccupied most kings, if not the peaceful Solomon, and which engaged the attention of the prophets—though there is a later reference, "the battle is not to the strong" (9.11).

Still, in this book's constant and recursive enlistment of paradox—as though to illustrate the self-frustration of thinking—the role of the king, too, receives the test of reversal: "Better *is* a poor and a wise child than an old and foolish king" (4.13). This dictum momentarily and permanently gives the lie to prosperity from four other directions: poverty, youth, lack of royal authority, and wisdom. And for the next three chapters, down to 7.20, the point of view reverses, becoming that of a subject, not a ruler.

The recurrent phrase peculiar to Ecclesiastes, of which the first occurrence is quoted above, "there is no new thing under the sun" (1.9), insists on a long view and a recapitulative control. Put in the mouth of a dramatized king, it evens out all the political turbulence of the prophets. Later, "a wise man's heart discerneth both time and judgment" (8.5) is an overarching summary that combines two conceptions central to the prophets, a view of the dominance of time and a reminder of the inevitability of judgment. The poor wise man, whose wisdom delivered the little city from siege (9.13–14), offers a schema that provides a structure reminiscent of events under which the prophets operated, without invoking their time contour. Then, too, this whole picture undoes the prophetic sense of recompense: the wise man does deliver the city, but no one remembers him. At the same time, in contradiction to such ongoing pessimistic events, the book's last words are of God's judgment on good and evil, returning to the tonic note of all prophets: "Let us hear the conclusion of the whole matter: Fear God, and keep his commandments: for this *is* the whole *duty* of man. For God shall bring every work into judgment, with every secret thing, whether *it be* good, or whether *it be* evil" (12.13–14). This is not the first mention of piety in the book. The term "good" here picks up other references, such as the "see good" of 2.24 and 3.13 and "enjoy the good" in 5.17. Still, these uses of "good" imply more "benefit" than they do "righteousness."

For all its underlying singleness of emphasis, Ecclesiastes, as many commentators stress, envisions a distant God and a faltering that comes through as wrapped in contradiction. At the same time, this book is more open-ended than is the simply prudential book of Proverbs. The applications of its significations are more sweeping, and its view of power structures more commanding, if also pessimistic. Instead of Proverbs' prudentially bounded application to specific, homely circumstances, Ecclesiastes envisions an unbounded constraint on circumstance: "For in much wisdom *is* much grief: and he who increaseth knowledge increaseth sorrow" (1.18). Like Proverbs, it distinguishes between the wise man and the fool, but unlike Proverbs it also, contradictorily, allows for the nullification of the difference between them: "For *there is* no remembrance of the wise more than of the fool for ever; seeing that which now *is* in the days to come shall all be forgotten. And how dieth the wise *man*? as the fool" (2.16).

The notion that "man cannot utter it" (1.8) goes beyond the notion that there is nothing new under the sun. The repetitions, including that of words such as *hevēl*, "vanity," play on their subincantational, subpoetic nature. All in turn are connected with, and contrasted to, the lack of remembrance. The much-repeated *hevēl*, indeed, puts the physical and the mental into implicitly contrastive conjunction, since it means "empty breath." And Charles F. Whitley points out the extension of the sense of this word to theological falsity in Deuteronomy 32.21, where in the plural it means "not a god," and in Jeremiah 8.19, where it is coupled with idols.[4]

Constantly are contradictions both built up and subverted. The notion that "he who increaseth knowledge increaseth sorrow" (1.18) is implicitly contradicted by the pervasive sense that humankind cannot know anything. Yet this book shows an overall certainty-in-weariness, as well as a concluding resolution to the divine will. In line with Proverbs' injunction against strange women, the "Convener" offers a super-Proverbial rejection of ensnaring women, who are "more bitter than death" (7.26). "My wisdom remained [literally, "stood up," *ʾāmdāh*] with me" (2.9) implies that the disillusionment works *beneath* the wisdom.[5] Chapter 7.1–7 offers a whole series of paradoxes that follow the non-paradoxical statement "A good name is better than precious ointment," *tov šēm mi šemen tov* (7.1). This simple aphorism is sealed and emphasized by two pairs of words in chiasmus, near rhyme, and paranomasia.

"My heart rejoiced in all my labor, and this was my portion of all my labor" (2.10). The sense of "labor" (*ʿamāl*, "hard toil"), a frequent notion in Ecclesiastes, here rests on a contradiction, since labor—in another dimension, the curse of Adam—is not usually linked to a yield of joy. "Eat drink and be merry" in 8.15 is repeated at 9.7. Joy offers a sort of blanket: "In the day of prosperity be joyful, but in the day of adversity consider: God also has set one over the other" (7.14). On the other hand, beauty serves as an obfuscation (3.11).

The notion of profit, *yītrôn*, and its lack, a financial metaphor, serves as a refrain: "There is no profit under the sun" (2.11). But then comes a turn, "wisdom excelleth folly, as far as light excelleth darkness"(2.13), a proverbial verse. And still another turn comes: "one event happeneth to them all" (2.14). An ethics of pleasure is offered again and again (2.24–26; 3.11–13); and yet, in a run of similar statements, it is said that "Sorrow is better than laughter" (7.3).

"To every *thing there is* a season" (3.1). In context, this notion recapitulates and widens the cyclical, neolithic base, picked up in the plant cycle of 3.2, to include philosophical elements. The word rendered "season," *zemān*, implies an appointment and so a conjunction of forces. "A time to every purpose under the heaven" expands this and sets the conception of "purpose" (*ḥepheṣ*, also "desire" or "pleasure") in a context where, if fulfilled, it will only be temporary, depending inescapably on a conjunction of events. And this aphorism introduces a whole run of paralleled contrasts:

> To every *thing there is* a season,
> And a time to every purpose under the heaven:
> A time to be born, and a time to die;
> A time to plant, and a time to pluck up *that which is* planted;
> A time to kill, and a time to heal;
> A time to break down, and a time to build up;
> A time to weep, and a time to laugh;
> A time to mourn, and a time to dance;
> A time to cast away stones, and a time to gather stones together;
> A time to embrace, and a time to refrain from embracing;
> A time to get, and a time to lose;
> A time to keep, and a time to cast away;
> A time to rend, and a time to sew;
> A time to keep silence, and a time to speak;
> A time to love, and a time to hate;
> A time of war, and a time of peace.
>
> (3.1–8)

These contrasts are interwoven with each other structurally, and they can be variously matched in their densities of simple presentation.[6]

At the extremes of life, a resemblance obtains between man and beast (3.18). But this only serves to widen the view. As André Neher says, "The thought of [Ecclesiastes] appears larger than that of Job. Injustice is not only social and moral, it is biological. It is not just with relation to man that the question is posed but with relation to the universe, where man shares with other elements the free privilege of being."[7]

In this vastness, the safe course is the prudential one of the mean to which Proverbs adheres and which, in that vein, Ecclesiastes echoes: "Be not over much wicked, neither be thou foolish: why shouldest thou die before thy time?" (7.17). "Be not righteous over much" (7.16). "Better is a handful with quietness than both hands full with travail" (4.6). As in Proverbs, the wise/foolish antithesis keeps coming up, governing specific recommendations, notably in chapter 5. If, as it happens, the fool sometimes does better, sometimes does worse, and sometimes does the same, this alternation at once holds and leads back to the "all is vanity" refrain (10.1–18). Yet events keep transcending this distinction: "Oppression maketh a wise man mad"—that is, "makes a fool of him," *yehôlēl* (7.7). There is "one event to the righteous and to the wicked" (9.2), and there is no further differentiation of fate between the sinner and the righteous, in the face of the "event," death (*miqreh*, "encounter," "chance," "fortune"). Death is oblique here, as it is in 6.2 where the prudent, industrious person amasses all and a stranger gets to "eat" it.

Seen at this angle, the Convener's counterprudential principle sweeps through all achievements: "The race *is* not to the swift, nor the battle to the strong, neither yet bread to the wise, nor yet riches to men of understanding, nor yet favor to men of skill; but time and chance happeneth to them all" (9.11). And yet this uncertainty can be inverted to a prudential principle: "Cast thy bread upon the waters: / For thou shalt find it after many days" (11.1). "Two *are* better than one" (4.9) reduces an elementary principle of cooperation to the bare bones. "Let thy words be few / For a dream cometh through the multitude of business" (5.2–3). In these words, a prudential principle is shadowed by something that suggests a wholly different one involving dreams, as is found in the principle soon adduced that could cover the whole book, "For in the multitude of dreams and many words *there are* also *divers* vanities: but fear thou God" (5.7). "He that observeth the wind shall not sow, / And he that regardeth the clouds shall not reap" (11.4) seems to recommend practical, not contemplative, life. But the focus at once moves to the inscrutability of God, with a hinge on "spirit," *rûaḥ*: "As thou knowest not what *is* the way of the spirit, *nor* how the bones *do grow* in the womb of her that is with child: even so thou knowest not the works of God who maketh all" (11.5). Thus this book weaves between certainty and uncertainty, gradually composing a structure of meditative coping.

As J. A. Loader well expresses, "In the Book of Quohelet we find neither a logical development of thought nor a loose collection of aphorisms."[8] If "wisdom," *ḥokmah*, is a form, it undergoes unique manipulations at the hands of this writer, who stretches between an emphatic verse parallelism and a prose that still lightly retains the antitheses of this verse, going well beyond the loose concatenations of Proverbs, in form as well as in doctrine. The retention of the proverbial form as a base while composing an extended run is a particular achievement, given the tendency for proverbs in most cultures to be presented in discrete series, as well as to be anchored in the merely prudential.[9]

In many of these passages, there is an effect of subparallel fluidity and adaptiveness that stands out against the stark schematism of runs such as 3.1–8, quoted above. A far more open set of conflations comes in the final chapter:

1   Remember now thy Creator in the days of thy youth,
While the evil days come not,
Nor the years draw nigh, when thou shalt say,
I have no pleasure in them;
2   While the sun, or the light, or the moon,
Or the stars, be not darkened,
Nor the clouds return after the rain;
3   In the day when the keepers of the house shall tremble,
And the strong men shall bow themselves,
And the grinders cease because they are few,
And those that look out of the windows be darkened,
4   And the doors shall be shut in the streets,
When the sound of the grinding is low,
And he shall rise up at the voice of the bird,
And all the daughters of music shall be brought low;
5   Also *when* they shall be afraid of *that which is* high,
And fears *shall be* in the way,
And the almond tree shall flourish,
And the grasshopper shall be a burden,
And desire shall fail:
Because man goeth to his long home,
And the mourners go about the streets:
6   Or ever the silver cord be loosed,
Or the golden bowl be broken,
Or the pitcher be broken at the fountain,
Or the wheel broken at the cistern.
7   Then shall the dust return to the earth as it was:
And the spirit shall return unto God who gave it.
8   Vanity of vanities, saith the Preacher;
All *is* vanity.

9 And moreover, because the Preacher was wise, he still taught the people knowledge; yea, he gave good heed, and sought out, *and* set in order many proverbs. 10 The Preacher sought to find out acceptable words: and *that which was* written *was* upright, *even* words of truth.

11 The words of the wise *are* as goads, and as nails fastened *by* the masters of assemblies, *which* are given from one shepherd. 12 And further, by these, my son, be admonished: of making many books *there is* no end; and much study *is* a weariness of the flesh. 13 Let us hear the conclusion of the whole matter: Fear God, and keep his commandments: for this *is* the whole *duty* of man. 14 For God shall bring every work into judgment, with every secret thing, whether *it be* good, or whether *it be* evil. (12.1–14)[10]

The static and recursive posture of all that has gone before in Ecclesiastes opens out expansively here and attains a marvelous luminosity. This culmination approaches the intensities of the prophets as it breaks enigmatically into metaphor, borrowing and condensing their images and themes. The social-process vision of the second chapter is here transmuted so that the society and the body become versions of each other. In the first verse, "the years draw nigh, when thou shalt say, / I have no pleasure in them" comes to a cosmic, prophetic sweep of sun, moon, and stars, clouds and rain. It broadens to a public setting; first from a dwelling, "the keepers of the house," then to strong men and grinders, then back to the house of dark windows and shut doors. All these visualizations in their range line up lightly under the rubric of "evil days" and "no pleasure" in the first verse, an unemphatic but definite case of staircase parallelism that continues in the lowness of the sound of grinding, the quick response to the (enigmatic) "voice of the bird," the decline of the daughters of music, and the ensuing fears, cresting in a run of further images that are at once lucid and profound.

This dwelling on fear is interrupted but also continued underground, as the staircase continues, with the sinister undercurrent of verses five and six, which have traditionally been read as a metaphor of the body, as a sort of "white hotel," to borrow the title of a striking novel. "The almond tree shall flourish" sounds positive and pleasurable, the sort of agricultural fertility that accompanies restoration in the prophets, since "flourish" here means "blossom" and almond blossoms are white. But this subdued metaphor is usually taken to figure the snow-white hair of the aged body, since the almond tree flowers in January. In this light, the grasshopper figures the feeble legs of the aged. These identifications also carry out the "evil days" and "no plea-sure" of the first verse, prefiguring the boldly direct summation at the turn of this run, "and desire shall fail." That phrase may indeed signal the cessation of a desire that is sexual.[11] But in this context, it must be still more comprehensive than that, since the "long home" of the par-alleled next line indicates death.

The lines roll on to finalities: "Then shall the dust return to the earth . . . and the spirit . . . unto God" (12.7)—a repetition with variation of "goeth to his long home" (12.5). So, too, "the mourners [who] go about the streets" (12.5), because they will be vocal, transform the sounds and music of the fourth verse, suddenly and sadly opening the streets on which the doors were shut. The mourners, indeed, and the "daughters of music" (12.4) strike across the gamut of sound in the city, where such sounds come at times of extreme collective expression, for celebration or for sorrow. "I will cause the noise of thy songs to cease" (Ezek. 26.13) is an oppressive warning. In Ezekiel, too, musical appurtenances, "tabrets and pipes" (28.13), climax a passage in which jewels and other precious objects are enumerated, the list of instru-ments an echo to the singing of the previous chapter (27.25).

In Ecclesiastes 12, all this reference to aging and death thus inverts the time focus of this chapter's first verse, "Remember now the Creator in the days of thy youth." This warning reverses the connection be-tween youth and vanity in the immediately previous verse, "childhood and youth *are* vanity" (11.10). Between the first of these references here and the final one, the sequence both reverts to the almond tree and cli-maxes in images that are also possible allegories of the failing body— the images of the silver cord, the golden bowl, the pitcher, the fountain, the wheel, and the cistern. These images, like the flowering almond, are externally beautiful while of ominous signification, setting up a con-tradiction internalized in the structure of the image between the tenor of its reference and the vehicle of the metaphor that moves the under-lying contradictions of the book into the resolution of a realized, dis-cordant concretization. These four lines of 12.6 in their parallelism strikingly repeat and vary each other.

Their intensifications have already been stretched out, as it were, in "long home" (12.5), where "long" is *ʿōlām*, a word that means "of long duration," "of great antiquity," and "forever." It is the term used for the "rock of ages" in Isaiah 26.4, and it is hard not to see these senses all converging, or at least hovering, in the uses here in Ecclesiastes. The riddle of the word is well conveyed in the sense of "long duration" rather than "eternal" chosen by the King James translator: "He hath made every thing beautiful in its time: / also he has set the world [*ʿōlām*] in their ["its"] heart" (3.11). In the parallelism of this earlier passage, "world" translates *ʿōlām* and therefore matches "time," *ēt*, itself a recurrent term in Ecclesiastes. It is as though the beauty enduring in transience envisioned by the last chapter had been anticipated by this maxim, endowing the temporary beauty with an eternity at its heart. Elsewhere, *ʿōlām* is rendered "forever," in "the earth abideth forever" (1.4), "For *there is* no remembrance of the wise more than of the fool forever" (2.16), "whatsoever God doeth it shall be for ever" (3.14), and "neither have they any more a portion forever" (9.6). The word is also used in the plural against the idea of newness:

Is there any thing whereof it may be said,
See, this is new?
It hath been already of old time [*ʿōlāmîm*]
Which was before us.

(1.10)

Since the "long home" indicates a final destination after wandering, the word "home" itself may faintly include an assertion, even so late in time, against the tents of what had once been a nomadic society. The use in this passage (12.5–6) of the "silver cord" and the "golden bowl" is the only one in the Bible, though silver and gold are standard honorifics of fullness and luxury, often paired throughout the Old Testament; the pairing has the effect of an expected parallelism, but cord and bowl are not so paired. *Ḥevel*, "cord," occurs otherwise in utilitarian contexts, whereas *gûllah*, "cruse," or "bowl," is a container for oil used as an honored shape for the globes atop the pillars of the Temple (1 Kings 7.41–42). *Šaqed*, "almond," is a desired shape on which other types of bowls are fashioned (Exod. 25.33; 37.19–20). The nut itself is a delicacy associated with its blossoming, ordinarily, but not here if the blossoming figures the white hair of the aged. The *galgal*, "wheel," is not the luxurious wheel used by kings for chariots, the *ʾōphan* that figures as a symbolic entity in Ezekiel, but again a utilitarian object. For the wheel to be broken means that water cannot be hauled up from the cistern, (*bôr*, "well" or "pit"). Such water sources are a necessity, but also a welcome locus of desire, in the dry desert country of much of the Holy Land. The pitcher, *kad*, shares in that association and suggests such a simple but abundant gift as the water-bearing pitcher brought forward by Rebekah at the well (Gen. 24.15).

The indirection and indeterminacy of the almond tree image, standing for the white hair of the aged body, is lightly laid over the external details of white blossoms, silver cord, golden bowl, pitcher, fountain, and the rest. There is, in fact, a kind of displacement at work, since the run of the verse seems to be voicing a seamless continuity from the ceasing of the grinders because they are few, and the daughters of music brought low, to the almond tree. There is no indication, other than the break for the verse about fear, that the almond tree shifts into a vehicle whose tenor is not a place of habitation but a body. In the continuity, the change is stronger from the darkened windows and the doors shut on the streets than from the daughters of music to the almond tree. And all these details fit easily, in a sort of super-pastoral, into a scene of gradually fading delight. The almond tree, in context, suggests a yard or garden where it is planted, something that the image of the grasshopper reinforces. And, indeed, for the grasshopper to be a burden suggests the kind of plague of grasshoppers in the dire words of other prophets like Nahum—an evocation that will point up how delicate the shading of sorrow is for this grasshopper.

The silver cord and the golden bowl come through as the decorations of an almost paradisal interior, the sort of home to which "man goeth" in the previous verse (12.5), where there are, to be sure, mourners in the streets. But in sequence the tonality of the silver cord and the golden bowl can be initially felt as superseding the mourning—though actually silver cord and golden bowl reinforce the mourning, if they are taken in the much-displaced figuration of the dying body. So, too, the pitcher and the fountain, the wheel and the cistern, taken in themselves belong to the same orderly scene. But they are swept up, always gently, to issue in the "dust" of the next verse (12.7). The displacements of the figuration, the shift to the body with the almond tree, and the deep discrepancy and obscurity of the relation between tenor and vehicle, all heavily mute the *memento mori* of these lines and distance their echo of a prophetic threat, here generalized and dissociated from the collective public life envisioned by the prophets—except, again, it is a busy, harmonious, gradually fading public life that carries the vehicle here.

The poetic force and effect in the final chapter push beyond and below the patterns of contradiction and resolution earlier in the book. The images have driven the speaker's contemplative act deeper than mere contradiction. Here the recurrent contradictions have been transformed into images that have a fullness and splendor to them, while ultimately they signify transience and loss, a vision that manages to figure loss without engendering nostalgia. The profound transmutations here both repeat and, in a different key, resolve the enigmatic signification of these indirections.

"Vanity of vanities" in verse 8 ties the knot with the long-range refrain, much repeated from the beginning.

The speaker "sought . . . words of delight [*haphes*, translated "acceptable words"]" (12.10) is a metalinguistic turn on his earlier uses of "delight" (including the first verse of the chapter). Words, then, may delight, even if the years do not. Yet this contradiction does not fall away. "Of making many books *there is* no end" (12.12) cancels even that delight. The conclusion puts everything under the judgment of God. As the speaker has already said, in an overriding notion presented earlier, "That which is far off and exceeding deep, who can find it out?" (7.24). This statement of ignorance is, at the same time, a statement of affirmation, as though the Voice from the Whirlwind in Job had been uttered not by God but by Job himself.

7

The Pressure of History in Zechariah and Daniel

First Zechariah

THE CHAPTERS OF First Zechariah (1–8), while not losing sight of
the prophet's orientation toward God in moral leadership over the
people, exhibit a temper put at some remove from collective social
stresses by the generations of exile under Babylonian and Persian rule.
This prophet can, as it were, adapt the spatial orientation of Ezekiel by
taking it for granted. Consequently the prophet's vision begins with his
situation in a low valley, and it unfolds more loosely and relaxedly,
without the firm hierarchies of Ezekiel, to say nothing of the intensities
of Jeremiah. This prophet's attention is on restoration, immediate and
ultimate. Like his contemporary Haggai, Zechariah prophesies at the
rebuilding of the Temple (Ezra 5.11) under Darius I, 520–518 B.C.E., who
confirmed and reaffirmed the original decree for its restoration promul-
gated by Cyrus (Ezra 6).

The prophet looks back somewhat peacefully to the old ways, un-
stressfully evoking the symmetry of old and modern troubles between
prophets and people by recalling the old situation. "Be ye not as your
fathers, unto whom the former prophets have cried, saying, Thus saith
the Lord of hosts; Turn ye now from your evil ways and *from* your evil-
doings: but they did not hear, nor hearken unto me, saith the Lord. Your
fathers, where *are* they? and the prophets, do they live for ever? But my
words and my statutes, which I commanded my servants the prophets,
did they not take hold of your fathers? and they returned and said, Like
as the Lord of hosts thought to do unto us, according to our ways, and
according to our doings, so hath he dealt with us" (1.4–6). Here the old
triangle of forces, God-people-prophet, is redescribed and evoked again
as a cyclical pattern of some assurance, because the people possess

those forces in a remembered background. There is no outward collective action they can take until the permitted restoration, which stands on the horizon.

This arrangement entails the loss of the tremendous directness of Ezekiel and his predecessors. It is activated through an intermediary, the angel. "What seeest thou?" the prophet is asked by the angel (4.2), and the dialogue between God and the prophet is organized consistently through the angel, who is identified with the man on the horse in the very first vision. As Christian Jeremias points out, here the angel has the mediating role that in earlier prophets the prophet himself occupied. The angel now stands between the prophet and God.[1] Soon he will be joined by a second angel (2.3). In chapter 3, there is an intermediary, too, and another figure: Joshua and Satan join the stage, facing the Lord. And still the text offers a constant, rather static conspectus of the moral universe, a stasis that reflects the fact that the Chosen People have long been subdued inside the Persian empire. In the command for orderly priestly management (3.6), there are no crosscurrents of prophetic stress. The prophet experiences and projects the quiet of a peaceful existence: "In that day, saith the Lord, shall ye call every man his neighbor under the vine and under the fig tree" (3.10). And when God says "not by might and not by power but by my Spirit" (4.6), there is a removal, again, from counterforces and an internalization not only towards vision but effectually away from the people. The pacification takes on symbolic actualization when the mountain becomes a plain before Zerubbabel. As the prophet says, "they [those who go toward the north country] have quieted my spirit" (6.8).

The command diligently to obey the voice of the Lord (7.16) involves no stresses. And the ritual, somewhat formalized in its reference (7.1–3), loses the stresses of Isaiah and Jeremiah. We hear of fasting in the fifth month, ritual laws, speaking to "the priests and prophets." When this prophet asks "should I weep in the fifth month . . . as I have done these many years?" (7.3), the Lord replies that they did so seventy years on their own behalf. Once again, the Lord is quoted as adducing earlier prophecy: "*Should ye* not *hear* the words which the Lord hath cried by the former prophets?" (7.7). True justice, mercy, and compassion toward a brother are again enjoined, and they *didn't* hear (7.9–

10). All this is put in the past, rather than as a moral condition in the present.

This is a "night vision," something like a dream though not characterized as a dream. In this, it differs from the visions of Ezekiel or the interpreted dreams in Daniel. Again, unlike the situation of Ezekiel and Isaiah, this vision is not given a stressful, pointedly framing location. The mystery of the location of the night vision is, as it happens, blurred in a single word, here translated "bottom," *meṣûh*: "he stood among the myrtle trees that were in the bottom" (1.3). The location of the prophet is fused with the location of the vision, and the "bottom" is indistinct enough to suggest both a valley and the depths of the sea: a valley, because that is where the myrtle trees that are used for ritual purposes might grow; and the bottom of the sea, by correlation with other uses of the word in the Old Testament.[2] However, "valley" does make sense here, while the reading "the deep," seductive for its figural intensities, introduces insoluble complications when it is joined with horses and myrtle trees.

For that which appears to the prophet, the intensive words "vision" and "dream" are not used; instead, it is the minimal one, "see," *rāāh*. Each time the prophet simply "lifted up his eyes" and described what he saw. The visions simply occur and are coordinated in their series; if the series is counted as seven, it unemphatically rings on a hieratic number. Jeremias sees a symmetry in the "cycle" of the seven visions. Yet, whatever their patterning may be, all are somewhat skimpily presented. As Jeremias observes, the "signification [*Deutung*] repeatedly comes through only an incomplete unveiling of the visualized image."[3]

This first vision comes abruptly:

> I saw by night, and behold a man riding upon a red horse, and he stood among the myrtle trees that *were* in the bottom; and behind him *were there* red horses, speckled, and white. Then said I, O my lord, what *are* these? And the angel that talked with me said unto me, I will show thee what these *be*. And the man that stood among the myrtle trees answered and said, These *are they* whom the Lord hath sent to walk to and fro through the earth. And they answered the angel of the Lord that stood among the myrtle trees,

and said, We have walked to and fro through the earth, and behold, all the earth sitteth still, and is at rest. (1.8–11)

The angel, the myrtle trees, the horse—this is a singular, almost pain-
terly vision, its visual dimension underscored by this presumably low-
lying terrain and by the quickly recapitulative specifications of color.
This specification tends to smooth allegory at this point into a plain
vision, away from the sorts of structure brought to bear on visions in
Isaiah, Jeremiah, Ezekiel, and Daniel—or later here, as the text transposes into allegory, with the four horses, the measurement of Jerusalem
(a simplification of Ezekiel), the vesting of Joshua (3.5), the eyes on the
stone (3.9), the candlestick (4.2) and olive trees (4.3), the flying roll (5.1–
4), and the woman explicitly allegorized as "wickedness" (5.7–8). The
horses return in the next to last vision. Now the color, more fully amplified, is assigned recursively to four chariots, "red, black, white, and
grizzled-and-bay" (6.2–3). They give way to a final vision, "the man
whose name is the Branch [*ṣemaḥ*]" (6.12; referred to also at 3.8), who
is to rebuild the Temple.

There is no concern here to dramatize the separate visions situationally, as is done in Jeremiah, with its parables, or in Daniel, with its
interpreted dreams. And the language that introduces each of them employs similar formulas. So both the absence of situational coding and
the repeated similarities of introductory phrasing point to the concate-
nation of these visions, and commentators have put them into various
orders. Moreover, while offering a sequence among themselves, they
spread the present of seeing into a broad past, present, and future.

These figures differ in complexity and in referential set. The myrtle
trees suggest a settled *locus amoenus*, but the horses open this scene out
to the military and the territorial, while the rider-man-angel insists on
the God-centering of the picture. This vision introduces and frames
God's declaration of jealous vigilance (1.14–15) and countervailing
mercy (1.16).

In the second vision (1.18–21), four horns alternate strangely with
four "carpenters" who destroy rather than build. The horns recall the
past: "These *are* the horns which have scattered Judah" (1.21). Milos Bic
points out that the horns in context here must have eschatological signification and that horns, in any case, are symbols of power among the

Sumerians and Akkadians that represent the king and sometimes his deification.[4]

The third vision (2.1–5) turns to the future, to a man "with a measuring line in his hand" (2.1) who will measure Jerusalem for rebuilding. "Measuring" evokes the active sense of proportion and order that is a component of human activity from early paleolithic times on.[5] The key dimension of architecture and city planning now becomes the focus, simplified from the elaborate preparations in Ezekiel (chapters 40–48) but comparably messianic. This restored city will have order and abundance, "towns without walls for the multitude of men and cattle therein" (2.4). But at the same time, it will be fiercely protected and triumphantly glorified, "For I, saith the Lord, will be unto her a wall of fire round about and will be the glory in the midst of her" (2.5).

A prophecy of restoration in the city leads to the fourth vision (3.1–10), of Joshua the vested high priest standing over against Satan. This descendant of the last high priest before the exile is characterized by an intense, proverbial expression as "a brand plucked out of the fire" (3.2). Joshua, if he remains faithful, shall be fortified by the Branch and by the stone with seven eyes. Here, while the Branch signifies a savior through a simple fertility symbol, the seven eyes upon the stone condense many significations. Seven eyes are significant and so are stones. To bring them together wrenches interpretative possibilities, both confusing and broadening them.[6] Differing from each other, the branch and the seven-eyed stone differ (except for the repetition of seven) from the likewise discordant elements of the fifth vision: the candlestick with seven lamps and seven pipes that present restoration in the form of lights for worship; and the two olive trees on either side of the bowl atop the lamp that root the restored worship in a seasonal fertility. In this vision, turning the mountain into a plain for Zerubbabel runs together the measuring plummet, the candlestick, and the olives, as well as the golden pipes and the golden oil (4.10–14). The Lord answers to a question that the two golden pipes emptying out are "the two anointed ones," *benē ha yiṣhar* (4.14), literally, "the sons of oil," an unusual phrase which insists on their figuration through the pipes, since the regular term for such figures, and for anointing, produces the word "Messiah," "the anointed one." And the wrenched, quasi-allegory turns the two priests, Zerubbabel and Joshua, into simple indicators of their holy function: they are golden pipes transmitting an equivalent of the oil they receive.

In a further vision (5.5–9), the identification of Israel's guilt as a woman, a traditional notion from Hosea through Jeremiah, is further emblematized in the figure of the woman sitting on an ephah, a "bushel" or measure of grain from the harvest. The ephah is "their resemblance [ʿênām, literally, "eyes," "appearance"] through all the earth" (5.6). "And, behold, there was lifted up a talent of lead: and this *is* a woman that sitteth in the midst of the ephah. And he said, This *is* wickedness. And he cast it into the midst of the ephah; and he cast the weight of lead upon the mouth thereof. Then I lifted up mine eyes, and looked, and, behold, there came out two women, and the wind *was* in their wings; for they had wings like the wings of a stork: and they lifted up the ephah between the earth and the heaven" (5.6–9). The suspension between earth and heaven points to a stable, inclusive order. The woman as an emblem guarantees survival just because, contradictorily, she stands for destruction; she has been turned from threat to reminder. And once again each of the elements here is conventional—the ephah with its lead seal, the woman, the two women who carry her off, the stork with its wings. It is the collocation that jars and puzzles an interpreter—woman and ephah and stork—as well as the action—the storklike women flying with the ephah. They are on their way "to build it a house in the land of Shinar, and it shall be established, and set there upon her own base" (5.11)—a permanent reminder of Babylon, the country of powerful evil.

The eighth vision (6.1–8)—or seventh, as they are variously counted—fills or repeats and varies the first, where at the start there was a rider on a single horse, then several horses. Chariots from mountains of brass are pulled across the heavens (chapter 6). These numerous horses are identified as "spirits of the heaven," coming forward to fill out a spiritual mission, to "quiet my spirit," as is said of the horses that go toward the north country (6.8). Covering both north and south, they are geographically comprehensive as well as spiritually effective. The mountains of brass point also to a heavenly origin.[7]

The roll flying through the air in the seventh vision is the curse, a sort of negative fact of life (5.2–4). The roll will go into the house of him who steals and him who swears and "consume it with the timbers thereof and the stones thereof." Wood and stone are here comprehensive; nothing will be left of the house. The strangeness of the action, a roll destroying a house, makes it total, a preparation for the Isaiah-like moral perspective of chapters 7 and 8, a vision of retribution and fulfillment. The relation between visions and moral-political imperatives is sealed in the succinctness of all these visual presentations.

Past is the history of Judah, present are visions taking over for the interdynamics of a relatively powerless present life, in order to foreground Judah's restoration in the future. This messianic future hovers over the text, which gradually and persistently reverts away from vision with quotation of promises from God: "The Lord shall comfort Zion" (1.17). "And the Lord . . . shall choose Jerusalem again" (2.12). This messianic force increases as the visions succeed one another, culminating, after the actual night visions, in the broad restorative and millennial predictions of chapters 7 and 8. When Joshua is crowned and the Branch comes, he will be "counsel of peace between them both [Joshua and the Lord]" (7.8). At the return to Zion, "Jerusalem shall be called A city of truth; and the mountain of the Lord of hosts, The holy mountain" (8.3). Longevity, a new notion of emphasis for the prophets, will become common (8.4); and at the same time, "the streets of the city shall be full of boys and girls playing in the streets" (8.5). "If it be marvelous in the eyes of the remnant of this people, . . . should it also be marvelous in mine eyes? saith the Lord of hosts" (8.6). Here a holy society is depicted in a few strokes, to be realized around the building of the Temple, according as they "hear these words by the mouth of the prophets" (8.9). Now new fasts are decreed at several months (8.19) and not just at the fifth month, as in chapter 7. Many cities, and finally the nations, will seek the God of the Jews (8.20–22). A messianic state will effectually have been realized.

Second Zechariah

Chapters 9–14 of Zechariah have long been understood to be by a separate hand. The association of the two parts of Zechariah together, then, was done primarily on thematic grounds. At the beginning of chapter 9, the text breaks emphatically into verse. Suddenly, "the burden of the word of the Lord" introduces an apocalyptic mingling of salvation and affliction (9.1). The writer at once "prophesies" as a future (9.2) what must be past to him, the devastation of Tyre by Alexander in 332 B.C.E.—whereas the events of the first chapters take place almost two centuries before, 520–518. The apocalyptic cast grows stronger, picking up a central theme of chapters 7 and 8 that conclude First Zechariah: the king shall rule from the sea and be sent to the ends of the earth (9.9–10). This involves a messianic kingdom, echoing one important theme in Second and Third Isaiah, though the meld of events and the tonality are different here:

And Tyrus did build herself a stronghold,
And heaped up silver as the dust,
And fine gold as the mire of the streets.
Behold the Lord will cast her out,
And he will smite her power in the sea;
And she shall be devoured with fire.

(9.3–4)

This prediction about Tyre is more succinct and summary than the comparable but much more lengthy prediction about Tyre in Ezekiel, chapters 26–28, and the same holds for other predictions of Zechariah. Even though the verse is oriented immediately on Alexander's conquest of Tyre and other Philistine cities, it does not direct its production of Israel's triumph at a specific set of events.[8] There is an angling that is almost anamorphic between sharpness of focus and obscurity of application. Israel will not, in fact, take over Philistia at any time: the historical and the apocalyptic do not move into convergence.

The imperial center is unannounced, but the text feels its pressure. In the prophecies about the Nations in chapters 9 and 10, more emphatically than the prophecies about them in other prophets, a direct connection to the Messiah is asserted. However, the messianic possibility stands at hand in the prophetic repertoire not only for application to the Israelites but also to other nations. Third Isaiah is comparably inclusive, while First Isaiah juxtaposes the Assyrian kingdom of a dire present to a messianic future for his people (10.5–12.6), expanding in the more usual lengthy census of other kingdoms (chapters 13–23). Insofar as Israel is a nation, it is exposed to the crux of its similarity to other nations and to a lack of virtue that may lead it to imitate them or worship their gods. But the similarity works two ways; under steady influence and the mysterious inclusiveness of divine favor, the other nations, too, may come to spiritual fulfillment—as they may also, more usually and expectedly, suffer overthrow and destruction, like the Nineveh to which Nahum directs his prophetic utterances. Amos begins with predictions of dire events for the nations, culminating with Israel (chapters 1–2). Jeremiah 46–51 and Ezekiel 25–32 open out in the prophecies that catalogue the fates, preponderantly disastrous, of other peoples. Such persistent inclusions imply the extent of God's power as they fortify the prophetic message with a range of exemplary tales.

Throughout Second Zechariah, there is a mingling of war, triumph, and peace, fertility shading over to fruitful rain in chapter 10. Soon there is an evocation of Exodus all over again (10.11). Egypt and Assyria fall, and in their affliction something like the end of the world is envisioned. As it has entered the parable of the staffs, the text both draws near to history, in a further allegory of the shepherds, and takes on an opacity, since the allegory is overridden by the structure of the parable.[9]

> And I will feed the flock of slaughter, *even* you, O poor of the flock. And I took unto me two staves; the one I called Beauty, and the other I called Bands; and I fed the flock. Three shepherds also I cut off in one month; and my soul loathed them, and their soul also abhorred me. Then said I, I will not feed you: that that dieth, let it die; and that that is to be cut off, let it be cut off; and let the rest eat every one the flesh of another. And I took my staff, *even* Beauty, and cut it asunder, that I might break my covenant which I had made with all the people. And it was broken in that day: and so the poor of the flock that waited upon me knew that it *was* the word of the Lord. (11.7–11)

The leaders of the people, here identified with the prophets, fall one after another: "Three shepherds also I cut off in one month" (11.8). These shepherds are the prophets, but what the phrase means leaves some ambiguity. Wilhelm Rudolph cites thirty-four different interpretations for it.[10] In this parable of the two staffs, Beauty and Bands, the complicated history is only insinuated. The symbolism is intermittent.

The next chapter begins with a recapitulation of the Creation but only to begin a litany of destruction for other peoples. Afflicted with mourning and separation (12.11–14), the Israelites will, at the same time, be restored as a "fountain" washes away their sin (13.1). At that moment, the prophets themselves are "smitten," and the prophecy recycles back to the fate given figural form in the shepherds of the previous chapters. Now the prophet as a "foolish shepherd" takes over (11.17) and is threatened: "Woe to the idol [or "evil," *elîl*] shepherd / that leaveth the flock!" This foolish or "evil" shepherd is marked by a neglect and hostility toward the flock. He neither tends the sheep nor heals them but devours them (11.15–16).

Cataclysmic events are foretold but as forerunners of the great, final restoration. Ritual sustains order; the Israelites are enjoined to keep Succoth and Tabernacles. Those who do not worship get no rain, a simple retribution. Further, they will get the plague, as happens equally with Egypt (14.16–18). An instability dominates the final stages here predicted. Two thirds die, but one third becomes a remnant tested and refined like gold (13.8). On the one hand, the prophets will be "ashamed every one of his vision" (13.4). On the other hand, they will be false prophets under an unclean spirit and will pass out of the land. Mysteriously, the prophets are squelched (13.2).

The House of David now becomes the prominent center of prophecies. An earthquake will cleave the Mount of Olives into "a very great valley" (14.4). From there, they will flee in refuge to the "valley of the mountains" (14.5). A light will be seen at evening (14.7), and "The Lord shall be king over all the earth" (14.9). A plague, hitting Jerusalem first, will cause the physical dissolution of every man, woman, and child (14.12).

Then, after the punishment of those who do not worship at the feast of Tabernacles, there is an abrupt transformation into a future of universal holiness, characterized in the severe foreshortening of two verses (14.20–21): "In that day shall there be upon the bells of the horses, HOLINESS UNTO THE LORD; and the pots in the Lord's house shall be like the bowls before the altar." This returns to the key image of the first vision, the horses of First Zechariah. There are to be bells on the horses, a transformation for these military animals. Horses that have been a "thorn in the eye" for kings (Deut. 17.16) come finally into peaceful glory.[11] These are the animals that earlier in the text were cut off (9.10) and blinded (12.4).

"The pots in the Lord's house shall be like bowls before the altar." This messianic fulfillment comes suddenly, leaving behind the earlier depictions of the planning of the city, the architecture of the Temple, and even the orderly, worshipful society—except that here it offers a vision of the messianic city in the glint of just two objects, pots like bowls before the altar and bells on horses, both enhanced by consecration, the pots to a holiness of everyday life in which "all that sacrifice" shall partake.

Daniel

Legend

In the Book of Daniel, the span set by the first chapter, from before the fall of Jerusalem in 596 till the accession of Cyrus in 538, refers to a time preceding by four hundred years the writing of the book itself. For some times the book stays with actual past events, except for the prophecy of the mountain covering the earth (2.35) and the longer prophecy of the messianic kingdom (chapters 9–12). The first comprehensive interpreted dream, the image of the statue and its fate, does not prophesy the future; rather, it recapitulates the past of those four hundred years, down to the present rule of Antiochus Epiphanes (175–164), who is "predicted" by the Hebrew figure Daniel. Daniel is recounted as living in Babylonian and Persian times, some four hundred years earlier. Hence, the book mostly lacks the commanding pressure of the future orientation of the major prophets, although it imitates the form, and it does not stay with the long-range focus that later dominates Revelations, wholly set in an eschatological future. Daniel presents a past as imagined future. Largely unlike Ezekiel and Revelations and more like the Book of Job, this book offers a prolonged fable of the past. In such a fable does it anchor its brief but startling apocalyptic utterances. It only extrapolates to the future—a future to the recounted past.

As for the allegorically conceived figures in chapter 7, the Ancient of days and the Son of man, they are set in the context of actual historical events: the ten horns are the Diadochi, the successors of Alexander, and the small horn is Antiochus Epiphanes. The focus is still on the proximate past moving towards the near present, and the future messianic dominion gets none of the elaboration presented later by Revelations or by Ezekiel's Temple earlier.

This remoteness from the recounted circumstances casts the book as a series of parables, and the parable-like force of the story is given a historicizing cast by the precise time-indications and situational depictions of the chapters. At the same time, the information it focuses on, coming in dreams and visions, is transmitted through legend-loaded images, which are themselves in turn keyed to a double reference, to both the moment within the story and the much later circumstances of the writer.

A legendary aura pervades the book. The mountain that covers the whole earth in the king's dream (2.35) is a widespread motif in the Near East. It is even found in the Odyssey: the kingdom of Phaeacia is so covered after Alcinoos has returned Odysseus home.[12] Mountains figure early in the religious iconography of the area; Zion is only a signal mountain, one among many. The great earth mountain was a charged place for the Egyptians and the Sumerians. The ziggurat itself is an artificial mountain.

The fact that the king has forgotten the dream, or pretends to have forgotten it, and threatens a disgraceful death to the interpreters who cannot recall it (2.5), puts it in the realm of *Märchen*, or fairy tale, where seemingly impossible tasks are assigned as tests. The story exhibits in a pure form the motif of the wise counselor from humble origins who executes prodigies of discrimination with some form of supernatural help. At the same time, an elaborate, powerful dialogue of negotiations ensues (2.13). Daniel is included in the (race-indiscriminate) extermination order. He says he will interpret if given time (2.16), and then the dream and its interpretation come through the mercy of God (2.18).

In this fable, the king finds Daniel and his cohorts "ten times better than all the magicians and astrologers that were in *all* his realm" (1.20). This glowing tribute, however, has an ominous side. The fairy-tale success is qualified by an intrigue that issues in another fairy tale. The

"Chaldeans"—here the king's wise men—accuse the Jews of not wor-shipping the king's golden image (3.8–13). There ensues a cross-exami-nation and then a condemnation of Shadrach, Meshach, and Abed-nego, Daniel's new deputies (who were included among the governors, having previously achieved a crossover from being wise men to becom-ing officials). The fire of the furnace into which these three are thrown kills those who cast them in but does not touch them or their clothing. The three walk in the fire along with a fourth, "the Son of God" (3.24). Nebuchadnezzar summons them forth and they come out unharmed (3.26). He blesses their God and identifies the Son as an angel, praising them that they "changed the king's word, and yielded their bodies, that they might not serve nor worship any god except their own God" (3.28). He decrees that anybody who speaks against their God shall be "cut in pieces and their houses shall be made a dunghill" (3.29)—the same threat he had issued for failed interpretation. He then promotes the three.

In the case of his second dream (4.10), some fifteen years later, the king now does not test Daniel by asking him to guess what he had dreamt; he tells it to Daniel and listens respectfully to the interpreta-tion. This dream of the World Tree enlists a motif common not only through the Near East but in other cultures as well, and the motif of the destroyed tree has a scriptural parallel in the tree that stands for Pharaoh in Ezekiel (31.2–18). The tree of Nebuchadnezzar's dream cov-ers the earth, giving food and shelter. In Daniel, it is not an eagle, as it was in Ezekiel, but a "watcher and a holy one come down from heaven" (4.13) that destroys it to the very stump. The tree, however, is not the king, in Daniel's interpretation, but rather the king's enemies. The king himself, in another fairy-tale motif, is to be driven from men, to act like a beast on all fours, and to eat grass for seven years—something that happens soon after the dream, which is thus, like the dreams of Pharaoh in Exodus, a prediction of the immediate future.

In the first year of the Persian Belshazzar (chapter 7), a dream is recounted out of temporal order from the portentous feast that spells the disastrous end of Belshazzar, recounted earlier in chapter 5. This time, it is Daniel, not the king, who has the dream. Daniel dreams of the four beasts who "come up from the sea" after "the four winds of the heaven strove upon the great sea" (7.2–3). Legendary motifs abound here, too. Yet the presentation modifies them, and the legends are not simple. On the one hand, the great sea, too, is loaded with legend; as Mathias Delcor says, "Biblical literature has preserved the memory of the abyss and of the sea that receives monsters, notably Leviathan, and that is a symbol of evil forces which only Yahweh can tame."[13] On the other hand, Daniel characteristically sets up or implies modifications on such legends. Norman Porteous, writing about the sea and the beasts in this passage, has this to say about chapter 7: "It must be recognized that whatever reference to the creation is intended is not made explicit. It is true that the expression 'the great sea' would probably suggest to a reflective reader that *tehôm* or abyss upon which order had to be imposed when God created the universe. The creatures which are represented in the vision as issuing successively from it, however, do not bear any notable resemblance to the monsters of the creation myth, either in appearance or function, but are intended rather to symbolize the brutal nature of the empires with which the Jewish people had had to do in the course of the last few centuries of their history."[14] And these four beasts, unlike those of Revelation, are applied to the same four successive empires, in the past to the writer but still in the future to the persona Daniel, that were already figured in chapter 2.

Figurative Structure

By his dreaming, the Babylonian king Nebuchadnezzar, rather than the prophet, serves as the intermediary for the first vision, which comes in chapter 2. The dreams of Pharaoh that Joseph interprets have the same pattern of relations, but Joseph, unlike Daniel, has not gone through the training of a professional seer. Rather, he has risen in service, and his dreams refer just to Egypt. The dreams in the book of Daniel are comprehensive, involving the entire kingdom in the person of the king, his history, and his future. The dreams that Joseph interprets in Genesis are simpler: The butler dreams of a vine and grapes, the baker of baked meats on his head, inverting the relation of agriculture to herding, since one might expect the butler, rather than the baker, to dream of meats; a pattern that is reminiscent of the fact that it was Abel, not Cain, who presented the meat offering that one might associate with the killer. The two dreams of Pharaoh devolve upon simple fertility, the dream of ears matching the agriculture of the butler's vine dream, and the dream of the fat kine and the lean kine matching that of the baker and his meats. Moreover, all these dreams present not phases but a simple up-down alternation, the first set alternating salvation and death, the second set alternating fat years with lean years. They do not involve the complexities of governance figured in Nebuchadnezzar's dream.

Daniel links advisorship to his training as a mage; he is accorded power, where Joseph independently volunteers advice about the lean years. It is this counsel, as well as his insight into the dreams, that gives Daniel overseership. While Joseph is untrained and humbled, he is also favored of God, whereas Daniel's relationship to both God and foreign king is much more structured and much more spectacular. At most, Joseph predicts the immediate future, whereas Daniel confronts dreams that are strange, comprehensive, and somewhat inward, especially that of Belshazzar's Feast. What stands in the scale for "Thou art weighed in the balances and art found wanting" (5.27)? Yet there are implied actions behind this assessment, whereas no reason is given in Genesis for why the butler is spared and the baker not. Moreover, in Exodus the delays also are random and not structured. Only when the king dreams, about two years later, does the butler remember Joseph's injunction to remember him. Here, as he was before Potiphar's wife and, even earlier, before his brothers in the pit, Joseph is at the mercy of events, somewhat random ones that are still derived from fluid power relations. Yet both Joseph and Daniel are caught in the large openings into deep patterns that dreams figure in many cultures.[15]

Daniel starts out with a structured explanation. Chapter 1 has told of Daniel's selection, along with other qualified captive youths, for elaborate training in "the learning and the tongue of the Chaldeans" (1.4). Daniel and the others are renamed by the eunuch-chief with whom he has got on a footing of "merciful kindness," *ḥesed*, (1.7–9). Acculturation proceeds through the Chaldean language for the children who already have wisdom and "understanding," *bîn*, a term used throughout the book. They are given three years of study with the goal of standing before the king. They are also given a special diet, the details of which receive much attention (1.5–15). The diet, a mere scholarship provision here, is transformed by the captives into a religious issue: they refuse it and substitute a pure diet of pulse and water. After the pulse and water diet, we hear for the first time of Daniel's selection, along with others who qualify (1.17); we may infer that his fidelity to the Hebrew God is the sufficient condition for his prowess as interpreter, even if the Chaldean training is a necessary condition.

In the king's first vision, the dream of the statue is a (spatialized) composite of dynamically temporal, divergent kingdoms (2.31–34). This is a composite human image whose "brightness *was* excellent . . . and form terrible" (2.31). Its head was of gold, its breast and arms of silver, its belly and thighs of brass, its legs of iron, its feet part iron and part clay. A stone not hewn by hands breaks the feet, and all the metal parts are broken together like chaff. The wind carries the chaff away, and "the stone that smote the image became a great mountain and filled the whole earth" (2.35).

Interpretation here turns time into space. Long successions undergo abrupt transitions and a varied sequence. The progressions from the gold head downward in space and forward in time unveil gradual declinations, as in the successive ages of Hesiod and Plato. The head of gold is interpreted to be the Babylonian empire; the others are the Median, the Persian, and the Macedonian, with the complications following upon the Diadochi governing the involved story of the iron-clay feet (2.41–43). "Mingling" is read as the alliance of the Seleucids with the Ptolemies.[16] The final kingdom is the messianic one, here not linked to other than the power of God; the prophetic dynamism is abrogated or wholly internalized. Reference is made to a permanent future: "And in the days of these kings shall the God of heaven set up a kingdom, which shall never be destroyed" (2.44); it will break others and stand as a mountain.

The political process here builds the dream into its actions. Right away, presumably, since any time indication is omitted, "Nebuchadnezzar the king made an image of gold. . . . he set it up in the plain of Dura" (3.1). In context, this is a counteraction on the part of Nebuchadnezzar. The gold of the statue, of course conventional, uses the same material as the head of the image in the dream. By making the whole statue of gold, the king in effect tries (vainly) to erase all the complications of the other materials and the disastrous sequences they signify. The dedication ceremony for this image (3.2) assembles a spectrum of rulers, listed twice, with repetitions that suggest the liturgical.[17] This group now includes the unnamed Daniel, since he is a governor (but again, not including the astrologers and magicians). Those assembled are commanded at the sound of music to worship the image and, if they fail (repeating the threat made in the interpretation of the dream), to be thrown into a "burning fiery furnace" (3.11)—a worse fate, but a repetition of the earlier penalty.

The story of Daniel in the lion's den (chapter 6) balances the story of the fiery furnace (chapter 3). In 7.6–27, it is an angel who interprets Daniel's vision. The Son of man here is transformed from his role in Ezekiel.[18] And again, the dream of the Son of man and the Ancient of days in chapter 7 complements, echoes, and balances the dream of the statue in chapter 2, as chapter 6 had done for chapter 3.[19] As Otto Plöger spells out the correspondences: "Therewith [the addition of the Son of man] is the essential advance offered with respect to Chapter Two, where neither in so many words nor metaphorically is Israel mentioned. Now, however, through Chapter Seven it is brought into play, and in the succeeding visions it is more and more pushed to the center, and indeed with relation to a particular historical situation, which in the vision is already noted in short form through the little horn. In that respect the much-discussed question whether a collective or an individual meaning is indicated for the significance of the *bar Enosh* [Son of man] loses its importance."[20]

The time shifts backwards without any indication that it had done so, whereas, up to this point, temporal sequence had been carefully indicated. There is a shift of key, much noted by interpreters, into what can loosely be called apocalypse, though much of the vision does not concern eschatological events. "In the first year of Belshazzar" (7.1), Daniel has the dream and the vision himself instead of interpreting them, getting them through an angelic intermediary, as Zechariah does, or undergoing dream-like revelations, like Ezekiel. Here the transformations of the four beasts translate essentially into straightforward political allegory: the eagle-winged lion, plucked and given the heart of a man; the bear eating three ribs from the flesh of his prey; the four-winged, four-headed leopard, which has "dominion"; and the fourth, unidentified except in its effects, "dreadful and terrible and strong exceedingly, and it had great iron teeth" (7.7).[21] This last beast has ten horns, and then another little horn grows, causing three horns to be plucked up by the roots, having "eyes, even the eyes of a man, and a mouth speaking great things" (7.8).

The text shifts to verse when it describes the Ancient of days sitting on his throne after the other thrones have been cast down:

> I beheld
> Till the thrones were cast down,
> And the Ancient of days did sit,
> Whose garment *was* white as snow,
> And the hair of his head like the pure wool:
> His throne *was like* the fiery flame,
> *And* his wheels *as* burning fire.
> A fiery stream issued
> And came forth from before him:
> Thousand thousands ministered unto him,
> And ten thousand times ten thousand stood before him:
> The judgment was set,
> And the books were opened.
>
> (7.9–10)

And, after a succinct prose account of the destruction of the largest beast and the disempowerment of the other three, the text reverts to verse for presenting the Son of man:

> I saw in the night visions,
> And, behold, *one* like the Son of man
> Came with the clouds of heaven,
> And came to the Ancient of days,
> And they brought him near before him.
> And there was given him dominion,
> And glory, and a kingdom,
> That all people, nations, and languages,
> Should serve him:
> His dominion *is* an everlasting dominion, which shall not pass
>   away,
> And his kingdom *that* which shall not be destroyed.
>
> (7.13–14)

Daniel, much troubled, consults for interpretation, which names the beasts as four kings. The puzzling fourth beast is the strangest; his ten horns are also ten kings—but he shall be destroyed "for speaking against the most High" and for thinking "to change times and laws" (7.25).

The text presents each sequence afresh, as though the lesson of the four successive kingdoms disappeared on presentation and had to be learned anew, given as it is from the different angles, in the different structures of the composite statue, the four beasts plus the horns, and the ram and the goat, and, finally, in the plainly mapped unallegorized intricacies of the last full statement (chapter 11). At the same time, what amounts to a judgment on Babylonian and Persian rule comes through in the dramatic narratives of the madness of Nebuchadnezzar and the catastrophic feast of Belshazzar. These are counterbalanced, respectively, by the saving of the three Hebrews in the fiery furnace and by the saving of Daniel in the lion's den. In both legendary historicized situations, the Hebrews come up whole and also uncorrupted, both actually and metaphorically, from a dangerous underground, a spatialized image of their position within these empires. In chapter 7, the four beasts present the kingdom of heaven as reflected by the kingdoms of this world, since the beasts come out of the great sea. Always, here and in chapter 2 and throughout, the same four kingdoms are recalled in their successive domination.[22]

The next vision (8.1) comes two years later, also in Belshazzar's reign (and, therefore, long before the cataclysm of the final banquet, narrated out of temporal order earlier in chapter 5). The vision takes place near Susa, in the extreme eastern part of the empire, far from Israel. A ram with bright horns, one higher than the other, pushes in all directions (8.3). Then a one-horned he-goat comes up to the ram and breaks into four divisions (8.5). Daniel says this lasted 2300 days of evenings and mornings (8.14), which R. H. Charles (ad loc) calculates as 1150 days of omitted sacrifices. This is a specific time that is both antiprophetic and too limited for apocalypse. The explicit historical interpretations are once again spelled out (8.20–27).

The type of allegory in chapter 8, where a ram opposes a goat, puts sequence into the format of natural animal rivalries and easy spatializations. The imagery is prophetic, but this apocalypse, again, imagines the future in the form of a simple parable. In this parable of a fictional time in the past, certain future events are predicted that, in fact, had happened in the recent past of the writer, told through a series of abrupt transitions; most notably, the predictions include the destruction of the Median-Persian empire (the ram) by Alexander (the goat) and the events after his death, down to the Seleucid solution of 301 B.C.E., without mentioning intermediary events until the persecution of the Jews by Antiochus Epiphanes (the little horn), beginning about 168. The "little horn" is a repetition from the previous vision. Here Antiochus initiates a religious persecution: "the daily *sacrifice* was taken away and the place of his sanctuary was cast down" (8.12).

Chapter 9 introduces a new ruler: Darius "the Mede" (as the writer calls him) rules over the Chaldeans. Daniel now measures himself by scripture—by a prior prophet, Jeremiah: "I understood by books the number of years" (9.2). And he stipulates seventy years, which will become seventy "weeks of years" after his devotions of preparation—an assimilation to ritual behavior of what was not so simply formalized in the earlier prophets. He prays, fasts, puts on sackcloth and ashes (9.3), confesses that "we did not listen to the prophets" (9.6), and utters the prayer that takes up verses 4–19. Thus, he moves his text to the second degree, by making reference mediately to the prophets as a fixed group in the past, whereas the prophets themselves referred directly to the urgent present. Here the Moses and Exodus of a legendary past are the model, Judah and Jerusalem the focus, as was often true for the earlier prophets.

In chapter 10, the last long vision comes about during the reign of still another ruler, Cyrus of Persia, the date again being uncertain but probably around 538 B.C.E.[23] This time the "word" (or "thing," *dāvār*) "was revealed . . . true," and it comes in the midst of Daniel's mourning and fasting (10.2–3). This time he is beside the "great river" (10.4).[24] The body of the man who appears to him is splendidly decked and "the voice of his words like the voice of a multitude" (10.7). Daniel sees all the others hide for fear—which means that the vision is not his alone. He, too, loses his strength: "my comeliness turned . . . into corruption" (10.8). He hears words, falls into a deep sleep, and then is set up on his hands and knees. The voice declares he is "a man greatly beloved" (10.12), and he is reassured against Persian opposition. But after all this elaborate stage-setting, the message is substantially the same as the message of chapter 8, effectually skipping again over the long period from Persian hegemony till the near past of the text and referring again to Alexander the Great in the transfer from "Persian" to "Grecian" rule (10.14–20). In the face of the revelation here, Daniel goes dumb, but an angel touches his lips and he speaks again (10.15–16), receiving and uttering "that which is noted in the scripture of truth" (10.21).

Historical Situations

The book projects steadily backward a Jewish role in the transfer from Assyrian to Babylonian rule and then to Persian. As André Lacocque remarks, "This *Sitz im Leben* is artificial."[25] That it is so casts the recounted history as a legend for contemplation rather than as a set of circumstances calling for action, as was the case in the earlier prophets; still less does the set of events undergo historiographic interpretation, as was true of those in Samuel and Kings or, in a different way, those in Genesis and Exodus. Under Nebuchadnezzar's rule, under Belshazzar's, and under that of later authorities, the external force remains substantially the same, exacting the condition that individual prayer must be maintained under pressure. Relations between mastery/subjection and private devotion remain constant.

"Daniel continued even into the first year of king Cyrus" (1.21). This expression introduces a historicizing keynote and presents a long, even time span, quite different from the abrupt dynamic of Ezekiel. Before long, there is a kind of power reversal in the area of religious worship. First, projecting on Daniel the pattern of Near Eastern deification of a powerful man, Nebuchadnezzar worships him (2.46). Then he praises Daniel's God (2.47). Next, he makes Daniel ruler "over the whole province of Babylon and chief of the governors over all the wise men of Babylon" (2.48). So Daniel, with respect to Babylonian power, has become at once subordinate and supreme, as well as melded into power because of his prowess at interpretation. And in chapter 4, after his restoration to sanity, Nebuchadnezzar's reaction is to praise Daniel's God.

At the beginning of the book (1.1–3), the fall of Judah is presented through the rhetoric of narrated history.[26] For the opening of chapter 3, also, the Septuagint version gives a precise time indication, "in the eighteenth year of king Nebuchadnezzar," an expression that locates the erection of this victory statue at the fall of Jerusalem, 587–586. However, the text also abounds in historical inaccuracies, as Charles points out.[27] The author of Daniel notably assigns Darius as emperor of a nonexistent Median kingdom, since the transition from Babylonian to Persian rule was direct, as is spelled out in Herodotus and other sources predating the book. But at the same time, the writer's sense of the large-scale historical sequences remains apposite, and sometimes accurately detailed, especially if one allows that "Persia" may be an unstated stand-in for the Seleucid kingdom of Antiochus Epiphanes some three hundred years later.

The historical conflations of this book undergo a complementary distinctness of phases. Belshazzar's feast in chapter 5, which doubles the prophet's message by a parallel writing on a wall, comes suddenly, without any mention of a lapse of about twenty-five years. There is continuity, though, in Belshazzar's use of the golden vessels for his feast, the same ones Nebuchadnezzar had taken from the Temple in Jerusalem (1.2). Here they are turned to idolatrous as well as secular ends: "They drank wine and praised the gods of gold, and of silver, of brass, of iron, of wood, and of stone" (5.4). This sacrilege leads directly to the mysterious handwriting on the wall: "In the same hour came forth the fingers of a man's hand, and wrote over against the candlestick upon the plaster of the wall of the king's palace" (5.5).

Once again the various soothsayers and wise men are unable to qualify for the offered rewards or read the writing on the wall. The queen, in an altered presentation of the court dynamic, remembers Daniel and has Belshazzar call him forth (5.10–12). Daniel refuses the rewards, recapitulates the glories and distresses of Nebuchadnezzar, and reads the writing, which this time is in no universal language but rather in a tongue that is obscure even to the other wise men. The message is like a proverbial distillate of the message of all the prior prophets, condensed to four (or three) words: *menē*, *menē*, *tekēl*, *upharsîn*. Each word, as condensed as a hieroglyphic, must undergo expansion and specification both to be understood and to be set in sequence: "MENE; God hath numbered thy kingdom, and finished it. TEKEL; Thou art weighed in the balances, and art found wanting. PERES; Thy kingdom is divided and given to the Medes and the Persians" (5.25–28). This is a sort of *hysteron proteron*, a schematized skewing of the time sequence, since weighing in the balance would come before finishing the kingdom, not afterwards, as it does in this text. Daniel gets the rewards anyway, and that night Belshazzar is slain and Darius takes over the kingdom.

"I, . . . even I, stood to confirm and to strengthen [Darius]" (11.1). The empire has now changed into a third rule, but Daniel still does not fall. For all his prophetic function, he is yet depicted as a high bureaucratic functionary within an alien empire. At this juncture, the book offers still another summary of the same history, from Darius to Alexander through the Diadochi down to Antiochus Epiphanes (11.2–12.4). The prophecy runs through many of the intervening successions and dynasties: the rivalries of the Seleucids and the Ptolemies, including a detailed account of power alternations ruler by ruler, with the Romans finally coming into the picture shortly after 200 B.C.E. (11.19–20). Again, what is actually past to the writer is fictionalized as the future to Daniel, in deep contradistinction to the prophets, who were involved in unfolding contemporary upheavals.

Fusions

The book of Daniel describes its own language, as it slips into Aramaic, as "Syriac" (2.14). This Near Eastern *lingua franca* erases the distinction between Babylonian and Jew while it is being used, since in the pen of the Babylonian it exemplifies the conquered as an intellectual conqueror and thus is symmetrical to the role of Greek at the time of writing (about 165 B.C.E.) and for the soon-to-come Septuagint version of the Book of Daniel. The universality of this language is assumed at the beginning of the fourth chapter: "Nebuchadnezzar the king, unto all people, nations, and languages, that dwell in all the earth; Peace be multiplied unto you" (4.1).

There is a fusion of tones in the vision following—Darius, Alexander, Antiochus Epiphanes are simple dominances that also imply a leveling. As the writer begins a verse praise of God (2.20–23), "he removeth kings and setteth up kings," an oblique constraint on the whole, as well as a prolepsis of the interpretation. Lacocque remarks, "The constant parallel established by Daniel between the celestial God and the mysterious character of history is remarkable."[28]

Lacocque points out that "the God of Daniel is always there where we least expect him to be: in a stone, a crematory oven, on a white-washed wall, or in a pit of ferocious beasts." Charles effectively underscores the progressive change in the role of religious worship in the book when he points out the differences between chapters 3 and 6: "In 3.1–30 the aim of our author was to direct his people how to act in their relations to *heathen religions* and to admonish them not to acknowledge or share in their worship, but rather to prefer death to apostasy. In this chapter it is his aim to enforce the duty of observing *their own religion*."[29]

But schematically, the theme of Darius and Daniel in the Lion's Den reprograms that of Nebuchadnezzar and the three Hebrews in the furnace. Here Daniel starts out as Darius's main deputy, with the consequent and politically predictable jealousies arising from the one hundred twenty princes under him. The only fault they can find in him as a line of attack is "the law of his God" (6.5). So they persuade Darius to set up a decree that, for a period of thirty days, anyone who "asks a petition of any God or man" except the king "shall be cast in the den of lions" (6.7). Here the preservation of features of Eastern rule—the deification of the ruler, the inviolability of his decrees even by himself—goes hand-in-hand with the miraculous, fairy-tale story. Daniel calmly prays according to his usual habit and is spied upon. The king, informed, tries to see a way out, but he has been caught in the trap of the inviolability of his decree. He says to Daniel, as he casts him into the den and before covering it with a stone and sealing it with the royal seal, "Thy God will deliver thee" (6.16), a prediction that fuses mockery and faith into a single utterance. The king fasts and spends a sleepless night, in a continuation of this curious three-way dynamic among himself, his officers, and Daniel, with God an overriding fourth. Rising early and running to the lions' den, he calls out to Daniel and is answered with the respectful formula, "O king live forever," sustaining the formula while countering it at once with the other, vastly larger power, "My God hath sent his angel, and hath shut the lions' mouths" (6.22). The gladdened king stays within the conditions of his power: he casts the accusers—"and their children and their wives"—into the den, where they are torn to pieces (6.24). Then Darius propounds another decree that concludes with a verse praise of the God of Daniel, in a standard prophetic run. Daniel "prospered in the reign of Darius and in the reign of Cyrus the Persian" (6.28).

Eschatology

At the departure of the Son of man in chapter 7, the emphasis now has turned to the future. As Lacocque says, "The *Endzeit* responds to the *Urzeit*, it assumes the same characteristics in that one vocabulary serves to describe them both."[30] The Son of man and the communion of saints take over a world already vivified in its subjection to primal typologies, the world sea, the four winds, and the general mythopoetic comprehensiveness of earlier legend. This transformation of primal material transforms the deep past into the deep future, *Urzeit* become *Endzeit*.

Under this onus, the writer says he encountered difficulty: "I sought the interpretation [*bînah*]" (8.15). Then there came "the appearance of a man," who in turn called for Gabriel to help him understand, "for at the time of the end *shall be* the vision" (8.17). A prophesied "king of fierce countenance" will understand "dark sentences" [riddles, *ḥîdôt*] (8.23). Daniel fainted but then recovered, rose up, and "did the king's business" (8.27).

Prayer, ritual, and recourse to the prophet Jeremiah now engage Daniel (9.1–20), with the result that "the man Gabriel whom I had seen in the vision" flew, talked, and offered understanding (9.21)—the understanding of what he had already read in Jeremiah, with a precise breakdown of how the seventy weeks of years would unfold. The "Messiah" (that is, "the anointed," in this case a high priest) is to come in sixty-nine "weeks" of years; but then he will be cut off, and the city

is to be destroyed. In all this, a fulfillment and the abrupt end in desolation are condensed into a simple, somewhat absolute sequence. The
persecutions of Antiochus Epiphanes in his last seven years, especially
168–165 B.C.E., are correlated with the Fall of Jerusalem and the Babylonian exile from 596 to 538—though the year calculations here remain
inexact as well as puzzling.[31]

The long account of 11.20–45 gradually shades into prophetic
phrasing, as though under the pressure of narrating these events and
as a tonal and figural prolepsis for the startling apocalypse of the last
chapter. Summaries are given of military actions, political intrigues,
and idolatries, all interacting, though too loosely to provide a historiographic interpretation and too specifically tied to secular events to have
the force of straightforward apocalypse, of wisdom exposition, or of
prophetic moral probing. The action does culminate in a pattern violation; the self-deification of Antiochus, his slighting of other gods, unfolds to idolatry in Israel itself: "he shall plant the tabernacles of
his palace between the seas in the glorious holy mountain [Zion]"
(11.45).

"And at that time shall Michael stand up" (12.1). The present gives
at once into a future of eternal eschatological vision:

> There shall be a time of trouble
> such as never was since there was a nation *even* to that same time;
> and at that time thy people shall be delivered, every one that shall
> be found written in the book
> And many of them that sleep in the dust of the earth shall awake,
> some to everlasting life, and some to shame *and* everlasting
> contempt
> And they that be wise shall shine as the brightness of the
> firmament;
> and they that turn many to righteousness, as the stars for ever and
> ever.
>
> (12.1–3)

Here the book comes into its own, changing, or rather, wholly harmo-
nizing the keys that have so far governed it. This vision of an after-
life has only partial, though distinct, forerunners in the prophets,
in Psalms, and in the cultures of associated Near Eastern peoples.[32] As

Lacocque puts it, in terms that apply almost wholly to this brief, but expansively inclusive, final chapter: "Then God had intervened in strength, today God is going to come in glory. The lesson of the Exile had been that the people's dereliction was a theophany at the same time—*galot* signifying both exile and revelation ('To whom has the arm of the Lord been *galah*?' Isaiah 53.1). When the Kingdom seems farthest off—it is closest."[33]

But then the book both brackets its own self-reference and refers to a kind of indefiniteness in this emphatic and eternal conclusion. There is the command to "seal the book" (12.4), which is this book, Daniel. Standing by the river, the linen-clothed angel declares "the end" and Daniel says "I understand not." But the book is now sealed "till the time of the end" (12.9), and the prophet receives only a sketch summary, rather than a definite resolution of his question, given in a kind of obliquity and future reference that "only the wise shall understand" (12.10).

Three associable worlds tend to converge here, as also at the end of Second Zechariah and in Third Isaiah: (1) a messianic perfect world unveiled in the future, (2) the apocalyptic final world of eternity, and (3) the typologically fulfilled world, the Old Testament revealed in the New. The first and second of these worlds come together easily: *Endzeit* and *Urzeit* become versions of each other. In the third world's typological figuration a present (in the future) will contain the past; and since it comes as a sort of predication, it leaves a universe between the old and the new.

The pressure of history applies to the present in the earlier prophets and then to the future, first immediate and then far reaching, in Isaiah, Zechariah, Ezekiel, and Daniel. All verge up to the prediction of a permanent, universal, messianic, and even apocalyptic future world. In this, however, the pressure of the present is always expressed in some form. Even in Ezekiel, who elaborates on the physical construction of the ideal apocalyptic city, there is a gradual transition into that state that differentiates his prophetic presentation from the end-of-the-world depictions in Revelations, where past and present have faded away before the tremendous events and embodiments that the writer announces.

In setting up correlations between Old Testament and New, the identification of actual events, difficult in the later prophets, becomes completely enigmatic. "Behold a virgin shall conceive, and bear a son, and shall call his name Immanuel" (Isa. 7.14). Interpretation would forever bog down over whether the ʿalmāh, the "young woman" or "virgin" of this passage from First Isaiah can refer at all to the Virgin, as it is taken in the New Testament (Matt. 1.23). If this expression is applied to Christ, there is still the question of whether it should be applied univocally, as though it were a unique event, or typologically, under the mother-of-the-hero type expounded by Lord Raglan and applied to Christian events by many commentators.[34] Just as markedly, the question remains of how we are to understand the thirty pieces of silver in Second Zechariah: "And I said unto them, If ye think good, give *me* my price; and if not, forbear. So they weighed for my price thirty *pieces* of silver. And the Lord said unto me, Cast it unto the potter: a goodly price that I was prized at of them. And I took the thirty *pieces* of silver, and cast them to the potter in the house of the Lord" (11.12–13). Marking this amount as the value of an injured slave (Exod. 21.32) deepens but does not redirect the typology. Even if this prophesy is misattributed to Jeremiah by Matthew (27.3–10), the conjunction of its terms and the circumstances of Judas's betrayal is extraordinary. For the non- or anti-Christian, the conjunction would be coincidental, while for the Christian it would be providentially confirming. Referring the thirty pieces to typology, reinforced by social convention, would only suspend it in the specifically unverifiable. Here "poetry" and "faith" are at a deadlock.

Such predictions, if they are the fulfillment of prophecy, open into an excess beyond the designations of the prophetic language, in which they both illuminate and fail to come clear. They cannot be brought firmly into visibility; they cannot be seen, and so they wholly exact, in the believer, an application of that "faith," which in the words of St. Paul "is the substance of things hoped for, the evidence of things not seen" (Heb. 11.1). Paradoxically, they cannot be made to designate the specific events at which they seem to be pointing. The endless attempts to make them do so, to turn Ezekiel or Revelations into Nostradamus, will always founder, of course, as the events unroll. And even sophisticated matchings of prophecy to particular networks of historical happenings, such as those of the devout statesman-writer Paul Claudel in his readings of Isaiah and Revelations, must somewhat base themselves on a misconception of the underlying structure of such utterances, for all the incidental aptness of such interpretations.[35]

At the heart of what is for us the paradox of a prophetic utterance about explicit certainties that will not be fulfilled lies a perpetual contingency. Contingency governed earlier prophets: disaster would overtake the Israelites and, indeed, was already in the process of doing so, only to grow worse if they did not mend their ways. In apocalyptic prophecy, dire and final disasters are matched by triumphantly total fulfillments, in a future declared to be certain that, however (paradoxically), continues to nest the prophetic contingency. To spell out the correspondences would flatten the implied contingency—and so would ultimately deny the correspondences. We are left with the correspondences in a magnificent vision that cannot really be tested either way. Its strength resides in its untestability; if it explicitly came to pass, it would be a report, a sort of newspaper of the future.

The typology of figural reference, however modulated, falls short of resolving the range of meanings forced in the apocalyptic passages of prophecy, because they themselves have transcended, by a tremendous leap, the conditions of their utterance. In the regular prophetic nexus of conditions—to bring up once again the performative situation I addressed at the beginning of this book—the triangle of forces among God, people, and prophet is constrained by an understood, conditional syntax. If the people behave a certain way, God will respond a certain way, and the prophet bears the message. The message conditionally tests the prophet, too: he is shown to be a true prophet not just because specific outcomes in the proximate future are accurately predicted, but because the prophetic message is rooted in the truth of an inalienable righteousness and justice. In the apocalyptic passages, this conditional syntax falls away—or rather it becomes coterminous with, and inseparable from, the essence of the whole hoped-for future. At the end of Ezekiel and Third Isaiah and Second Zechariah, more darkly at the end of Daniel and more mutedly at the end of Ecclesiastes, a permanent world of a final future is envisioned that will come about, it is asserted, no matter what. Revelations carries such expression to the ultimate concentration of a focus on nothing else.

That the conditional may fall away is correlatively hinted at in the prophecies about the Nations that are a staple constituent of prophetic utterance. These prophecies, from Amos on, move outside the conditional, except insofar as the fate of the Other in the destiny of Nations may serve as a warning to the Israelites. Unlike the Israelites, however, the Nations are not conceived of as able through piety to deflect their fate; even their conversion is simply in the cards. Nor does the prophet bear the message to them; the prophet only bears a message about them to the Israelites. That message remains differentially in the conditional mode, until it is transcended in the apocalyptic sweeps of prediction. These sweeps of prediction drop an exact correspondence to happenings in measurable time, as they drop the conditional, to constitute the fullest expression of prophecy.

Notes

Index

Notes

1. Introduction

1. Francis Brown, S. R. Driver, Charles A. Briggs, eds., *A Hebrew and English Lexicon of the Old Testament, Based on the Lexicon of William Gesenius*, Oxford: Clarendon Press, 1955, ad voc.

2. For an elaboration of the contrast between the prophets and poets of other traditions, see Albert Cook, "Prophecy and the Preconditions of Poetry," in *Soundings*, Detroit: Wayne State University Press, 1991, 44–56.

3. As Roland de Vaux says, "The Israelites worshipped a personal God who intervened in history: Yahweh was the God of the Covenant. Their cult was not the re-enacting of myths about the origin of the world, as in Mesopotamia, nor of nature-myths, as in Canaan. It commemorated, strengthened or restored that Covenant which Yahweh had made with his people at a certain moment in history. . . . It is important to stress that the Israelite cult was connected with history, not with myth" (*Ancient Israel*, vol. 2, New York: McGraw-Hill, 1965, 272).

4. George E. Mendenhall, "Ancient Oriental and Biblical Law," in *The Biblical Archeological Reader 3*, ed. Edward F. Campbell and David Noel Freedman, New York: Anchor, 1970, 21, 6–8. He also explains that

> Religious and legal obligations were not so closely identified in Israelite religion. This is to say that an act contrary to the will of the deity will be punished in ways which vary, of course, depending upon the concepts of divine action held by the community. Since the punitive acts of a god tend to be natural calamities such as plague, drought, and famine which strike the entire community, religious sanctions tend at least to reinforce, if not to produce, the concept of corporate responsibility which is a characteristic of the early stages of legal thought in the ancient world. Religious obligations tend then to become legal obligations, for the community will feel compelled to punish in order to protect itself from the divine wrath which does not single out the culprit alone for punishment. (4–5)

5. Mendenhall, "Ancient Oriental," 16.

6. George E. Mendenhall, "The Hebrew Conquest of Palestine," in Campbell and Freedman, eds., *Biblical Archeological Reader 3*, 109–10. Mendenhall continues:

> But the state could not create the biblical norms of personal relationships by power alone, and when the preservation of the state became the primary concern of official political and religious leaders, the exercise of power, unrestrained except by opposing power, became dominant, and the prophets had to predict its destruction. . . . Early Israel thus cannot be understood within the framework of traditional academic ideas about a primitive society gradually becoming urbanized, and therefore civilized. Its very beginnings involved a radical rejection of Canaanite religious and political ideology, especially the divine authority underlying the political institutions, and the Canaanite concept of religion as essentially a phenological cultic celebration

of the economic concerns of the group—the fertility cult. . . . the usual functions, authority, and prestige of the king and his court are the exclusive prerogative of the deity. So land tenure, military leadership, "glory," the right to command, power, are all denied to human beings and attributed to God alone. In this way, even the theological aspects of Old Testament religion represent a transference from the political to the religious. Not until David is the old Canaanite legitimacy of kingship reintroduced, but considerably modified at first by the entrenched Israelite system of religious values. (110)

7. Walther Zimmerli goes through the various interpretations from Heinrich Ewald onwards, providing a number of definitions himself in *The Law and the Prophets*, Oxford: Basil Blackwell, 1965. See also Werner H. Schmidt, "Die prophetische 'Grundgewissheit' " in *Das Prophetenverständnis in der Deutschsprachigen Forschung seit Heinrich Ewald*, ed. Peter H. A. Neumann, Darmstadt: Wissenschaftliche Buchgesellschaft, 1979, 537–64.

8. See Robert R. Wilson, *Prophecy and Society in Ancient Israel*, Philadelphia: Fortress Press, 1980; David L. Petersen, *The Roles of Israel's Prophets*, Sheffield: JSOT Supplement Series 17, 1981. See also Siegfried Hermann, "Prophetie in Israel und Ägypten," 515–36; Franz Hesse, "Wurzelt die prophetische Gerichtsrede im israelitischen Kult?," 394–404; and George Fohrer, "Bemerkungen zum neueren Verständnis der Propheten," 475–492, in Neumann, ed., *Das Prophetenverständnis*.

9. This statement was in effect powerfully interpreted by William Blake when he used it as an epigraph for his prophetic *Milton*. The force of this idealization is stressed by Heinrich Ewald, "Die Propheten im Leben," in Neumann, ed., *Das Prophetenverständnis*, 52–90 (75). Moses' declaration occurs in a context where seventy elders have prophesied, and he refuses effectually to forbid others to prophesy: "And the Lord came down in a cloud, and spake unto him, and took of the spirit that was upon him and gave it unto the seventy elders: and it came to pass, that, when the spirit rested upon them, they prophesied, and did not cease. But there remained two of the men in the camp, the name of the one was Eldad and the name of the other Medad: and the spirit rested upon them . . . and they prophesied in the camp. . . . And Joshua the son of Nun, the servant of Moses, one of his young men, answered and said, My lord Moses, forbid them. And Moses said unto him, Enviest thou for my sake? would God that all the Lord's people were prophets" (Num. 11.25–29).

10. Kenneth Dauber, "The Bible as Literature: Reading like the Rabbis," *Semeia* 31 (1985), 27–48.

11. Martin Buber bases the belief of the prophet on the developing interaction of prophet, God, and the people through their king. As he says of Isaiah, "What is this hope? Its original essence [*Wesen*] and its origin cannot be grasped if one starts with an 'eschatology,' from a teaching or representation of 'last things.' . . . its core belongs not to the edge of history where it flows into the timeless, but to its ever-changing center, the experienced hour and its possibility" (*Der Glaube der Propheten*, Zurich: Mannesse, 1950, 204).

12. J. L. Austin, *How to Do Things with Words*, Oxford: Clarendon Press, 1962.

13. Pierre Bourdieu, *The Political Ontology of Martin Heidegger*, Stanford: Stanford University Press, 1991, 57. See also *Language and Symbolic Power*, Cambridge: Harvard University Press, 1991.

14. Indeed, insofar as any achieved poetry always has some prophetic function, the intrication of poets into the power structure of their time is not to be characterized simply as "inequality." In Shakespeare's famous restatement of a topos from Horace, who was also complexly subjected to imperial rule, "Not marble nor the gilded monuments / Of princes shall outlive this pow'rful rhyme" (Sonnet 55).

15. Bourdieu, *Political Ontology*, 58, 67.

16. Pierre Bourdieu uses the Aristotelian-Thomistic term *habitus* to indicate the complex of prevailing acts and attitudes governing "practices" (*pratiques*):

The division into classes performed by sociology leads to the common root of the classifiable practices which agents produce and of the classificatory judgments they make of other agents' practices and their own. The habitus is both the generative principle of objectively classifiable judgments and the system of classification (*principium divisionis*) of these practices. It is in the relationship between the two capacities which define the habitus, the capacity to produce classifiable practices and works, and the capacity to differentiate and appreciate these practices and products (taste), that the represented social world, i.e., the space of life-styles, is constituted. . . . The habitus is not only a structuring structure, which organizes practices and the perception of practices, but also a structured structure: the principle of division into logical classes which organizes the perception of the social world is itself the product of internalization of the division into social classes. . . . This means that inevitably inscribed within the dispositions of the habitus is the whole structure of the system of conditions, as it presents itself in the experience of a life-condition occupying a particular position within that structure. (*Distinction: A Social Critique of the Judgement of Taste*, trans. Richard Nice, Cambridge: Harvard University Press, 1984, 169–72)

17. See Timothy Polk, *The Prophetic Persona: Jeremiah and the Language of the Self*, Sheffield: JSOT Supplement Series 32, 1984. For a counterexample, see Frederic Will, "Solon's Consciousness of Himself," in *The Generic Demands of Greek Literature*, Amsterdam: Rodopi, 1976, 73–84. Still, the self-consciousness of Solon and of such poets as Archilochus, Alcaeus, and Alcman does not extend to the record of specific interactive personal circumstances of the fullness offered by Isaiah and Jeremiah. And even so, the earliest of these references—in a different culture, to be sure—is later than Isaiah. Again, in Egyptian writing, the succinct personal references of Amenhotep, to say nothing of the chronicling boasts in king lists from Babylon and elsewhere, are a far cry from autobiography.

18. Scholars have tended towards the opinion that the later chapters of Micah have been edited in the postexilic period. However, the continued reference to the Assyrians would locate at least the reference, and perhaps the text as well, to the period 734–701 B.C.E. Here and elsewhere, I quote from the King James Version, arguably still the most forceful in English as well as reasonably accurate. I will note its fairly rare discrepancies from the most informed modern interpretation when these bear on my discussion. Those who are not familiar with it should note its practice of italicizing words for which there is no corresponding locution in the Hebrew text.

19. Hans Walter Wolff, *Micah: A Commentary*, tr. Gary Stansell, Minneapolis: Augsburg, 1990, 127, 135–36.

20. Delbert R. Hillers, *Micah*, Philadelphia: Fortress Press, 1984, 65.

21. Robert Alter, *The Art of Hebrew Poetry*, New York: Basic, 1985, 29. The centrality of repetition in the form of parallelism and the condensed intensities it allows lead to a variety of identifications between the first member and the second in the parts of a "bicolon," to use the term of Wilfred G. E. Watson. So Watson introduces the interesting supplemental category of "gender-matched parallelism." In the verse "His GLORY covered the HEAVENS / and the EARTH was full of his PRAISE" (Hab. 3.3), the first two capitalized nouns are masculine, the second two feminine. "All these elements—gender-matched synonyms, the verb, and the word pair and the verb—combine to convey the idea of completeness which fits in with the meaning of the couplet" (*Classical Hebrew Poetry: A Guide to Its Techniques*, Sheffield: JSOT Press, 1986, 31). Here, and even more so elsewhere, the pairings produce both contrast and identification, opening the door to internesting categories of verse-formal description. Attention to these formal properties of parallelism will yield a range of sets of identifications among the matched terms. So Stephen A. Geller, relying on the general studies of linguistic parallelism by Roman Jakobson, adapts his method to analyze the range of variants and transformations in biblical poetry. See *Parallelism in Early Biblical Poetry*, Missoula, Montana: The Scholars Press, 1979.

22. Benjamin Hrushovski, "Prosody, Hebrew," *Encyclopedia Judaica*, New York, 1971, 1200–1201; Alter, *Art of Hebrew Poetry*, 8–10. A summary of earlier discussions and much detail is given by George Buchanan Gray, *The Forms of Hebrew Poetry*, London: Hodder and Stoughton, 1915.

23. Theodore Robinson, *The Poetry of the Old Testament*, London: Duckworth, 1947, 30–41.

24. James L. Kugel, *The Idea of Biblical Poetry: Parallelism and its History*, New Haven: Yale University Press, 1981, 69. His discriminations are precise: "The clauses are regularly separated by a slight pause. . . . 'A is so, and *what's more*, B is so.' . . . it is the dual nature of B both to come *after* A and thus add to it, often particularizing, defining, or expanding the meaning, and yet also to harken back to A and in an obvious way connect to it" (8). "Interrelation and complementarity are often the whole point" (17). "Chiasmus in Hebrew . . . represents a decision *not to parallel* the word order of A" (19). "To state the matter somewhat simplistically, biblical lines are parallelistic not because B is meant to be a parallel of A, but because B typically *supports* A" (52).

Kugel does say that *mašal*, the formal proverb, may imply parallelism. Indeed, his whole argument is complicated, if not qualified, in the evidence offered by Gray: "But parallelism is characteristic not only of much in Babylonian and Hebrew Literature: it is characteristic also of much in Arabic literature. And the use of parallelism in Arabic literature is such as to give some, at least apparent, justification to the claim that parallelism is no true *differentia* [sic] between prose and poetry; for parallelism in Arabic accompanies *prose*—prose, it is true, of a particular kind, but at all events not poetry, according to the general opinion of Arabian grammarians and prosodists. Not only is parallelism present in much Arabic prose: it is commonly absent from Arabic poetry, *i.e.* from the rhymed and carefully regulated metrical poetry of the Arabs" (40–41).

25. Kugel, *Idea of Biblical Poetry*, 85, 93–94, 95.

26. Robinson, *Poetry of Old Testament*, 49–66. The rhetorical staples discerned by the form-critics can be seen as underlying these generic poems. As Fohrer summarizes some of them, "Bach has tried to analyze the demands for flight and for struggle, Horst the depictions of vision, Vetter seer-utterance, Wolff the bases of holy and

unholy utterances and the call to a folk-lament, Wurthwein cult instruction, and I the category of reports over the symbolic transactions of the prophets" ("Verständnis der Propheten," in Neumann, ed., *Das Prophetenverständnis*, 476).

27. Roland de Vaux, *Ancient Israel*, vol. 1, New York: McGraw-Hill, 1965, 74–76.

28. Richard S. Scripps (*A Critical and Exegetical Commentary on the Book of Amos*, London: S.P.C.K, 1929, 120) suggests a connection of fire in Amos to that mentioned in Deuteronomy (32.22) and Genesis (19.24), adducing analogues in Isaiah, Zephaniah, and Psalms. Scripps correlates the fire of the great deep in 7.4 to Babylonian legend (223).

29. Scripps, *Critical and Exegetical Commentary*, 143.

2. "The Burden of the Valley of Vision": Time and Metaphor in Isaiah

1. Brevard S. Childs, *Isaiah and the Assyrian Crisis*, London: SCM Press, 1967, 35–47.

2. Childs, *Isaiah*, 114.

3. Robert Lowth, *De Sacra Poesi Hebraeorum Praelectiones Academicae*, London, 1753. These types are well expounded and amplified in Robinson, *Poetry of Old Testament*, 20–46.

4. "Behold, he prophesied among the prophets, then the people said . . . Is Saul also among the prophets?" (1 Sam. 10.11).

5. Max Weber, *Das Antike Judentum* (*Gesammelte Aufsätze zur Religionsoziologie*, vol. 3), Stuttgart: Zechnall, 1922.

6. In addition to references in Isaiah, false prophets come into consideration in Mic. 5–6, 1 Kings 22.5–28, Amos 7.12, and Ezek. 13.19. Prophets, true and false, and questions about them are brought before the king in 1 Kings 22.6–9. Isa. 8.19 refers to "wizards that peep and mutter," *meṣaphṣephim ve ha maheggim*—like false prophets. Their language here is interestingly characterized as unrhythmic, as though their very rhythms were a giveaway to their lack of credentials. Of course, false prophets are a major theme in Jeremiah.

7. References to eyes are frequent in Isaiah, and such references are often indeterminate as to physical and spiritual vision. Especially arresting are the occurrences at 3.8, 5.21, 13.18, 22.1, 29.7, related notions like "wake up," and all the references to the vision of Isaiah.

8. Paul Grice, *Studies in the Way of Words*, Cambridge: Harvard University Press, 1989.

9. In this connection, see Cook, "Prophecy and Preconditions," 44–56, which I have adapted here.

10. The point about the similarity of their flight from Mesopotamia to Abraham's is made by P. E. Bonnard, *Le Second Isaie*, Paris: Lecoffre, 1972, 248–49. Bonnard also finds the reference to isles (coastlands) in Isa. 51.5 inclusive of other nations.

11. André Lamorte, *Le Problème du temps dans le prophétisme biblique*, Beatenberg (Switzerland): Editions Ecole Biblique, 1960, 37. Lamorte goes on to assert that there is an emphasis on completions both in the perfect used in the *vāv* consecutive (the "and" at the beginning of a biblical narrative sentence that has the effect of reversing the verb tense) and in the fact that it is consecutive. "In its nature as a perfect, it points to the positive character of the accomplishment. In its consecutive form it

confirms just the idea, implied in the main imperfect tense [which the *vāv* consecutive reverses to a perfect], of an appropriation of or a future realization of the announced fact" (67).

12. In Isa. 27.3, watering ("I the Lord will water it") is presented not as the usual reliable ongoing procedure but as something taking place "by moments," *regāʿîm*.

13. The word *beged* is used in speaking of spiderwebs in Isa. 59.6: "Their webs shall not become garments." This suspends the metaphor's effectiveness while continuing it. The metaphor resumes strength in 59.17, picking up reference to a series of effective garments:

For he put on righteousness as a breastplate,
And a helmet of salvation upon his head;
And he put on the garments of vengeance for clothing,
And was clad with zeal as a cloak.

3. Exemplary Intensities in Jeremiah

1. As Polk says, "Through his first-person speech Jeremiah enacts a prophetic identity of identification with both God and people. [There are] nuanced lines in the characterization. Representing each party to the other, Jeremiah is subject to an extraordinary tension. He . . . comes personally to embody the divine-human event such that his life becomes a vehicle for the event's interpretation. Jeremiah's life becomes his message" (*Prophetic Persona*, 125).

2. The image of the yoke is comparably adaptive: "For of old time I have broken the yoke," says God (Jer. 2.20). But then, commutatively, the people have acted perversely in the same mode:

But these have altogether broken the yoke,
And burst the bonds
Wherefore a lion out of the forest shall slay them.

(5.5–6)

This image becomes a figural action on Jeremiah's part: "Thus saith the Lord to me; Make thee bonds and yokes and put them upon thy neck" (27.1). Jeremiah is to send these to his own king and various foreign ones to show that the subjection of his people will last till such time as they accede to this condition, when it will produce a haven. God says, for "The nations that have put their neck under the yoke of the king of Babylon" (27.11), "I have broken the yoke of the king of Babylon" (28.2) and "I will break the yoke of the king of Babylon" (28.4).

3. Harold Bloom, *Ruin the Sacred Truths*, Cambridge: Harvard University Press, 1989, 15–17. Bloom quotes the rendering of Jeremiah 20.7 in Bright's Anchor Bible:

You seduced me, Yahweh, and I let you,
You seized and overcame me.
I've become a daylong joke,
They all make fun of me.

4. Joseph Blenkinsopp, *Wisdom and Law in the Old Testament*, Oxford: Oxford University Press, 1983, 48, 44.

4. "The Vision Is Touching the Whole Multitude": Vision and History in Ezekiel

1. On the similarities between Jeremiah and Ezekiel, see Walter Zimmerli, *Ezekiel*, vol. 1, Philadelphia: Fortress Press, 1979, 44–45.

2. Zimmerli, *Ezekiel*, 1:124–31, points out the many slippages one finds in trying to account for the connections between Ezekiel's figures and Near Eastern analogues. For the Near Eastern ambience of the individual figures themselves, he cites L. Dürr, *Ezekiels Vision von der Erscheinung Gottes im Lichte der vorderasiatischen Altertumskunde*, Würzburg: Richter, 1917. Further examples are given in G. A. Cooke, *The Book of Ezekiel*, Edinburgh: Clarke, 1936, 12–19, 29–30.

3. For these figures taken individually, says Cooke, "The symbolism of the faces is well explained by the Rabbis: 'man is exalted among creatures; the eagle is exalted among birds; the ox is exalted among domestic animals; the lion is exalted among wild beasts; and all of them have received dominion, and greatness has been given them, yet they are stationed below the chariot of the Holy One' Mdr. R. *Shemoth* 23 (on Ex. 15.1)" (*Book of Ezekiel*, 14).

4. In each case, I take these alternate, more scholarly, and modern renderings from Zimmerli's *Ezekiel*.

5. James Barr, however, argues that especially in the expression "word of the Lord," the sense "word" and the sense "fact" are not necessarily copresent (*The Semantics of Biblical Language*, Oxford: Oxford University Press, 1961, 129–40). Barr cautions generally against too intensive a reading of biblical words in specific contexts.

6. Zimmerli, *Ezekiel*, 1:17.

7. Apposite is Cooke's quotation from Nicolas de Lira (Prologue to the Works of Walafridius Strabus, Migne, *Patrologia Latina* vol. 113, 33): "Liber scriptus intus et foris: foris quantum ad sensum letteralem; intus vero, quantum ad sensum, mysticum sub littera latentem. [The book is written inside and out: outside with respect to the literal sense; inside, indeed, with respect to the mystical sense concealed beneath the letters]" (*Book of Ezekiel*, 35).

8. Zimmerli, *Ezekiel*, 1:156.

9. See Moshe Greenberg, "On Ezekiel's Dumbness," *Journal of Biblical Literature* 77 (1958), 101–5.

10. B. Lang, "Street Theater, Raising the Dead, and the Zoroastrian Connection in Ezekiel's Prophecy," in *Ezekiel and His Book*, ed. J. Lust, Leuven: Leuven University Press, 1986, 297–316. Lang sees Ezekiel's Valley of Dry Bones as echoing the dry bound of the Zoroastrian funeral grounds.

11. This chapter offers elements of both parable and metaphor, according to Horacio Simian-Yofre, "La Métaphore d'Ezechiel 15," in Lust, ed., *Ezekiel and His Book*, 234–52.

12. The same verb form occurs in 28.14, "walk [*hīthalāktā*] on the stones of fire," with a shift into metaphor perhaps cued by this intensive verb.

13. For further correlation of the prophecies about nations with the overall bearing of Ezekiel, see Lawrence Boadt, *Ezekiel's Oracles Against Egypt*, Rome: Biblical Institute Press, 1980; "Rhetorical Structures in Ezekiel's Oracles of Judgment," in Lust, ed., *Ezekiel and His Book*, 182–200.

14. Zimmerli, *Ezekiel*, 1:19.

15. Like others, however, Cooke attributes the change of persons to the conflation of different texts. See *Book of Ezekiel*, 3.

16. Cooke, *Book of Ezekiel*, 31.

17. For such extensibilities, see Emmanuel Levinas, *Quatre Lectures talmudiques*, Paris: Minuit, 1968, cited in "Judiciousness in Dispute, or Kant after Marx," in Jean-François Lyotard, *The Lyotard Reader*, ed. Andrew Benjamin, Oxford: Blackwell, 1989, 324–59.

18. This parallels an expression at Heb. 21.4.

19. Ellen F. Davis connects Ezekiel's dumbness and also the scroll-wafer to the recently developed predominance of writing in what had been an oral culture: "Ezekiel's dumbness is a metaphor for the move toward textualization of Israel's sacred traditions; the figure stands over all that follows to designate this prophet's career as a critical juncture in the history of revelation. . . . the edible revelation . . . comes to Ezekiel already as a text" (*Swallowing the Scroll*, Sheffield: Almond Press, 1989, 50–51).

20. De Vaux, *Ancient Israel*, 1:8. See also Cooke, *Book of Ezekiel*, 84.

21. Zimmerli, *Ezekiel*, 1:38.

22. For a systematization of God's relation with the people in this book, see Paul Joyce, *Divine Initiative and Human Response in Ezekiel*, Sheffield: JSOT Press, 1989.

23. Earlier (Ezek. 34.5–14), the betrayal by the shepherds is built into the verbal changes rung on the root *rā'āh*, "feed": *r'ôeh*, "shepherd," and *mīr'eh*, "pasturage."

24. Zimmerli says of this passage, "But it does not only provide the development of what is in itself a static vision, but shows, as already 1:1–3:15; chapters 8–11; chapters 40ff, that the prophet participates in the divine activity. . . . But then this is expanded into the two stages of the reconstitution of the body and the revival of this still dead body by the *rûah*. Certainly this expansion does not appear in any way unnatural, for it takes as its hidden model the process of the primeval creation of man as this is reported in Gen 2:7. . . . [Verse 37.1 is] fairly closely related to the beginning of the great vision of the new temple in 40.1ff" (*Ezekiel*, vol. 2, Philadelphia: Fortress Press, 1983, 257–59).

25. Zimmerli, *Ezekiel*, 1:27.

5. Sign, Song, and Prayer in the Dynamic Internality of Psalms

1. See Claude Lévi-Strauss, *Le Cru et le cuit*, Paris: Plon, 1964, 36–40.

2. The expression "new song" is characteristic of Psalms, occurring at 33.3, 96.1, 98.1, and 144.9. Otherwise, it occurs only once elsewhere in the Old Testament, Isa. 42.10.

3. Both readings are given in the Septuagint, where the Davidic ascription would contradict an exilic date. See J. J. Stewart Perowne, *The Book of Psalms*, vol. 2, London: Bell, 1893, 195.

4. *The Psalms*, ed. A. Cohen, London: Soncino, 1945, 449, briefly summarizes received opinion on the line. Charles A. Briggs revises the line in accordance with the translation of St. Jerome, which still leaves the paradox, "Thou hast magnified above all things thy word" (*Psalms: International Critical Commentary*, vol. 2, Edinburgh: Clark, 1907, 487). Perowne gives other citations for the sense "promise" but

says that "no particular promise is meant," which effectually revises the term back toward the lexical sense (*Book of Psalms*, 2:496).

5. See Othmar Keel, *Die Welt der altorientalischen Bildsymbolik und das Alte Testament*, Zurich: Neukirchen, 1972, 158–62. Keel discusses and reproduces images of cliffs with reference to Jerusalem and other places.

6. Keel, *Die Welt*, 186.

7. "The verb . . . is used of a sacrifice which is acceptable to God (Jer. 6.20; Hosea 9.4). His hope is accordingly that his meditation will find favor with Him" (Cohen, ed., *Psalms*, 343).

8. In Hebrew, particles and suffixes are often joined to the word, where in English they are given as separate locutions.

9. Briggs, *Psalms*, 2:414–19. Briggs prints a complete table of the recurrences of each of the eight terms through the twenty-two stanzas.

10. In the *tāw* stanza, "cry" (*rinnah*) is not repeated but the notion is, and the whole psalm, like others, constitutes a "cry." "Come near" (*qārav*) recurs from verse 150. The root for "understanding" (*bîn*) occurs in verses 27, 34, 73, 100, 104, 125, and 144. "Before" (literally, "to the face of," *lephnē*) is repeated in 168 and 170, while "face" (*panekha*) occurs in verses 58 and 135. "Supplication" (the root *ḥēn*) occurs in verses 29 and 161. "Deliver" (*nāṣāl*) occurs many times throughout the Psalms, though only once in this one. "Utter" (literally, "pour forth," *nāvʾā*, the root on which *nāvîʾ*, "prophet," may have been formed) is also radically endemic to the Psalms, though not repeated here; nor is "tongue" (*lašôn*). "My lips" (*śefātai*) is repeated in line 13; "teach" (*lāmād*), in lines 7, 64, 66, 71, 124, and 135; "sing" (*ʿanāh*, also "answer"), in lines 67 and 26; "righteousness" (*ṣedeq*), in lines 40, 62, 75, 106, 123, 137, 138, 142, 144, 160, and 164; "hand" (*yād*), in 73; "chosen" (*bāḥār*), in 30; "longed for" (*ʾāvāh*), in 20 and 40; "salvation" (*yešûʿāh*), in 41, 81, 94, 123, 146, and 166; "delight" (*šʿeašîm*), in 24, 47, 92, and 143 (constituting all but two of the uses in the Bible). "Soul" (*nepheš*) is repeated in lines 20, 25, 28, 81, 109, 129, and 167; "live" (*ḥayah*), in 17, 37, 40, 77, 88, 93, 107, 116, 149, 154, 156, and 159; "go astray" (*tʿāh*), in 110; "lost" (*ʾāvād*), in 95. The word "sheep" is not repeated, but it is certainly a much-used topos in Psalms, as it is in the Bible generally. "Servant" (*ʿeved*) comes up in 17, 23, 65, 84, 91, 122, 124, and 125, while "forget" (*šakaḥ*) comes up in lines 16, 61, 83, 93, 109, 139, 141, and 153. Put simply, the series of repetitions within this one psalm is remarkable for its density, range, and frequency, as a semantic and rhythmic amplification of the repetition of the eight words for "law" throughout.

11. See, for example, Augustine, *Enarratio in Psalmos*; Thomas Merton, *Bread in the Wilderness*, New York: New Directions, 1960.

12. S. R. Driver, *An Introduction to the Literature of the Old Testament*, New York: Meridian, 1956, 368.

6. Self-Reference, Prophetic Recursion, and Image in Ecclesiates

1. For a strong qualification of connections between Ecclesiastes and possible Greek parallels, see Oswald Loretz, *Quohelet und der Alte Orient*, Freiburg: Herder, 1964, 45–57. Loretz does adduce close parallels between some postures in Ecclesiastes and Egyptian and Babylonian texts.

2. De Vaux, *Ancient Israel*, 2:212.

3. The details of the correspondences with the books of Kings are analyzed by A. Cohen in his edition of Ecclesiastes, *The Five Megilloth*, London: Soncino, 1946, 116.

4. According to Charles F. Whitley, "Such references indicate that *hevel* denotes not merely what is vaporous and evanescent, but that which is without substance and false" (*Qoheleth: His Language and Thought*, Berlin: de Gruyter, 1979, 7).

5. J. A. Loader not only scrupulously lists the polarities in Ecclesiastes; he coordinates and structures them, sometimes into levels of self-redefinition. See *Polar Structures in the Book of Quohelet*, Berlin: de Gruyter, 1979, 8, 29, 37–38, 72–73.

6. See, for example, Loader, *Polar Structures*.

7. André Neher, *Notes sur Quohélét*, Paris: Minuit, 1951, 29.

8. Loader, *Polar Structures*, 8.

9. See Albert Cook, "Between Prose and Poetry: The Speech and Silence of the Proverb," in *Myth and Language*, Bloomington: Indiana University Press, 1980, 211–24.

10. The "prose" run here and continuing on to the last two verses could be reprinted as poetry, given its easy assimilabilty to being cast as a run of parallelism.

11. The word *seviyonah* is probably better rendered "caperberry," a stimulant to desire, as it is translated in the Septuagint, the Vulgate, and the Peshitta. See James L. Crenshaw, *Ecclesiastes*, London: SCM Press, 1988, 187.

7. The Pressure of History in Zechariah and Daniel

1. Christian Jeremias, *Die Nachtgesichte des Sacharja*, Göttingen: Vandenhoek & Ruprecht, 1977, 98.

2. According to Milos Bic, "The Hebrew expression *metsulah* . . . is otherwise fundamentally given the general rendering 'depth,' the actual depth of the sea. It has to do with the depth of the sea that has swallowed Pharaoh with his whole army (Exodus 15.5). There will Jonah be thrown (Jonah 2.4). Into it will the Lord cast all the sins of his people (Micah 7.19). There he has in early times performed his miracles (Psalm 107.24), and out of that place will he pull out his own (Psalm 68.23)" (*Die Nachtgesichte des Sacharja*, Neukirch: Erziehungsverein GmbH, 1964, 11–12). Bic adduces other citations: Neh. 9.11, Job 41.23, Pss. 69.3 and 88.7, and Second Zech. 10.11. He goes on to other associations with the great deep, beginning with the Creation therefrom in Gen. 1.21.

Many alternate readings for this probably corrupt text are summarized by Heinz-Günther Schöttler, *Gott inmitten seines Volkes*, Trier: Paulinus, 1987, 52; and Wilhelm Rudolph, *Haggai—Sacharja 1–8—Sacharja 9–14—Malachi*, Gutersloh: Gerd Mohn, 1976, 73–74. The Septuagint reading "in the shadows," *tōn kataskiōn*, does not clarify the interpretation.

3. Jeremias, *Die Nachtgesichte*, 68; see also 11–13, 61–71.

4. Bic, *Die Nachtgesichte*, 15–16. He also suggests that the number four may be connected to the Babylonian formula *Tsar kibratim arbain* ("king of the four regions of the world").

5. The significance of measure is well expressed by Michael Boughn, summarizing Alexander Marshack's paleolithic researches: "Some of the earliest known human artifacts . . . are bones incised with notches which measure or delineate the full cycle of the moon. . . . What shall we call these measures? Calendars? Astronomical records? Poems? Myths? Art? Spiritual texts? Their very undecidability and ambigu-

ity reveal an astonishing commonality of undertaking in the act of measuring" ("Measure's Measures," unpublished manuscript).

6. Rudolph, *Haggai*, 100–101, runs through some possibilities for the stone, such as a jewel in Aaron's breastplate (Exod. 28.17) or a building block for the Temple.

7. See Rudolph, *Haggai*, 123–24. The reference to brass is also possibly a reminiscence of the Babylonian sun god Shamash issuing from his brass gates. Visual representatons of Akkadian and other versions of such sun gates are reproduced and discussed in Keel, *Die Welt*, 17–20.

8. See Rudolph, *Haggai*, 176.

9. So Georg Fohrer characterizes this story, along with others, in *Studien zur alttestamentlichen Prophetie*, as cited in Magne Saebo, *Commentary on Zechariah 9–14*, Neukirchen: Neukirchen-Vluyn, 1969, 243–44.

10. Rudolph, *Haggai*, 206.

11. See Rudolph, *Haggai*, 239–40.

12. Zeus permits Poseidon to "hide the city round with a great mountain" (Homer, *Odyssey* 13.158).

13. Mathias Delcor, *Le Livre de Daniel*, Paris: J. Gabalda, 1971, 144. Delcor cites Isaiah 17.12–14; 27.1; Psalms 74.13–14; 89.10–11; 104.25–26. As he says, "According to the *Enima Elish* Tiamat gave birth to [various beasts]" (144). He further cites on this legend Otto Kaiser, *Die Mythische Bedeutung des Meeres, in Ägypten, Ugarit und Israel*, Berlin, 1959.

14. Norman W. Porteous, *Daniel: A Commentary*, Philadelphia: Westminster, 1965, 99.

15. For a survey of such patterns and their implications about "reality," Freud and Jung are, of course, commandingly apposite. For extensions of their interpretative methods about dreams in other cultures, see Wendy Doniger O'Flaherty, *Dreams, Illusions, and Other Realities*, Chicago: The University of Chicago Press, 1984.

16. Here I am following the commentary of R. H. Charles, *A Critical and Exegetical Commentary on the Book of Daniel*, Oxford: Clarendon Press, 1929.

17. See André Lacocque, *The Book of Daniel*, Atlanta: John Knox, 1979, ad loc.

18. See André Lacocque, *Daniel in His Time*, Columbia: University of South Carolina Press, 1988, 153–61. Lacocque speaks of the Son of man as "prophetic, messianic, kingly, priestly, and angelic" (155) and as offering a "bridge between the celestial and the terrestrial" (158).

19. For the details of these interrelationships, see Lacocque, *Book of Daniel*, 106–8.

20. Otto Plöger, *Das Buch Daniel*, Gütersloh: Gerd Mohn, 1965, 113.

21. The four beasts of chapter 7 are the same four kingdoms, with the horns as the Diadochi and the little horn as Antiochus Epiphanes. On the Near Eastern iconographic background, Lacocque quotes Elias Bickerman: "In Babylonian astral geography, lion, bear, and leopard respectively symbolized the south (Babylonia), the north (Media), and the east (Persia)" (*Book of Daniel*, 139, quoting Bickerman, *Four Strange Books of the Bible*, New York, 1967, 102).

22. For details, see Charles, *Critical and Exegetical Commentary*, 167–73.

23. See Charles, *Critical and Exegetical Commentary*, ad loc.

24. The author identifies this river as the Hiddekel, the Tigris, but since he is presumably in Babylon, it is more likely to be the Euphrates, according to Charles and others.

25. Lacocque, *Book of Daniel*, 24.

26. Charles, *Critical and Exegetical Commentary*, 5–7, describes in detail the imprecision of dating attributable to the writer's distance from the events.

27. Charles, *Critical and Exegetical Commentary*, 139–46.

28. Lacocque, *Book of Daniel*, 43.

29. Lacocque, *Book of Daniel*, 108; Charles, *Critical and Exegetical Commentary*, 146.

30. Lacocque, *Book of Daniel*, 122–23. Lacocque goes on to link the presentation here to its underlying Near Eastern archetypes: "As in the ancient cosmologies common to the whole Near East, the wind from the four cardinal directions stirs of the waters of the Primordial Sea to extract, in a fashion, potentionally terrestrial creatures from it. Between sea (v.2) and sky (v.13), there is a dialogue called earth. But, faithful to its genius, Israel 'demythologizes' this cosmology. The creatures born of primordial chaos are historical empires which may be defined—folllowing the canvas already encountered in chapter 2—as Babylonia, Media, Persia, and Macedonia. Furthermore, these empires, which at first glance reflect human greatness, are here only monsters more and more contrary to every human dimension." See also 129–32.

31. See Charles, *Critical and Exegetical Commentary*, ad loc.

32. For a summary, see Lacocque, *Book of Daniel*, 236–40.

33. Lacocque, *Book of Daniel*, 252.

34. For this census of the typological features of the birth and life of the hero, see F. R. S. Raglan, *The Hero: A Study in Tradition, Myth and Drama*, London: Methuen, 1936.

35. See Paul Claudel, *L'Evangile d'Isaïe*, Paris: Gallimard, 1951; *Introduction à l'Apocalypse*, Paris: Egloff, 1946; *Paul Claudel interroge l'Apocalypse*, Paris: Gallimard, 1952.

Index

Albert Cook is the author of twenty books of criticism, eight books of poetry, and translations of the *Odyssey*, *Oedipus Rex*, and Russian poetry. For many years, his theoretical criticism has focused on questions concerning the philosophical bases of the literary use of language. His most recent books are *The Reach of Poetry*, *The Stance of Plato*, and a volume of poetry, *Reasons for Waking*. A professor emeritus at Brown University, he lives and works in Providence.